The Romance of The Book

*For my parents,
Stewart and Natalie Brooks,
who always had books
around the house*

*''Books which are books
are all that you want, and
there are but half a dozen in
any thousand.''*
— Henry David Thoreau

The Romance of The Book

Edited by *MARSHALL BROOKS*

BIRCH BROOK PRESS

*ISBN: (hardcover) 0-913559-32-6
ISBN: (softcover) 0-913559-28-8
Library of Congress Catalog Card No.: 95-076146*

Designed, typeset & printed letterpress at:
      Birch Brook Press
      PO Box 81
      Delhi NY 13753
Write or call (212) 353-3326 for a
      free catalog of books & art.

Birch Brook Press and the editor wish to express
grateful appreciation to the following writers,
publishers and agencies for permission to reprint
the works listed:

JAN MORRIS for "Through My Guide-Books."

NEW DIRECTIONS, NEW YORK, for the excerpt from
The Books in My Life, by Henry Miller; and for
the excerpt from *Conversations with Kafka*, by
Gustav Janouch.

PETER OWEN, LTD., LONDON, for the excerpt from
Looking Backwards, by Colette.

RANDOM HOUSE, NEW YORK, for the excerpt from
The Autobiography of Malcolm X, by
Malcolm X and Alex Haley.

WIDE WORLD PHOTOS, NEW YORK, for the photograph
of the bombed library of Holland House, ca. 1941.

GORDON WILSON for "The Bookworm," from *Three
Stories* (Newton, MA: Arts End Books, 1980).

Second printing 1996

PREFACE

I am deeply indebted to the following friends and colleagues who took the time to make suggestions on what to include in this collection, and who even, in several instances, allowed themselves to be coaxed into writing pieces for it: Bill Costley, Janet Crosby, Thomas F. Connolly, Brenda Lyons, Jim McGinn, Ivy Tillman, and Fred Wilkins.

My profound thanks to Birch Brook Press, without whom there would simply be no book at all. They originated the idea for the book and, what's more, cast, handset and printed it letterpress — a demanding feat.

The following Massachusetts libraries and library systems were essential to my research: the Boston Athenaeum; the Boston Public Library; the Central Massachusetts Regional Library System; the Concord Free Library; the Newton Free Library; the Richard Sugden Library, Spencer, Massachusetts; and the Worcester Public Library.

Special thanks to Janet Greene, through whom I gained important library privileges at the Boston Athenaeum.

Bob Oliver scanned the cover artwork into the computer and skillfully enhanced the image so that it could be effectively turned into an engraving and printed via letterpress.

Stephanie Greene, my wife, not only tirelessly supported my research for this book but was generously willing to share her own writing for the good of the cause at a moment when — with two young sons afoot — time for her own work was limited to a precious few minutes per day.

In view of the wonderful involvement of all the aforementioned individuals and institutions, I hasten to add that any and all errors of fact and omission are entirely my own.

Readers should note that the styles of spelling and punctuation sometimes vary throughout this collection. Every attempt has been made to remain faithful to the original printed text which often reflect the spelling and grammatical preferences of another century or place. That said, it was sometimes necessary — in the case of some of the longer essays and, of course, the excerpts — not to include certain parts of a piece due to the material's lack of relevance and availability of space in this book. For an anthology assembled with the general reader — not the lamp-burning scholar — in mind, the editor and publisher felt this was a reasonable route to follow. An ellipsis (. . .) indicates where these necessary deletions occurred.

To everyone who patiently listened to me while I described and discussed this project, I extend my deepest thanks and gratitude.

—MB

TABLE OF CONTENTS

INTRODUCTION
Living Intensively with Books

THERE IS NO TELLING what you will discover in a book—a strand of hair; a paper clip; a postcard from the Grand Canyon; a catalog from the Eugenics Publishing Company, circa 1937 (offering *Sane Sex Life*, "Dr. Long's Masterpiece"); the autograph of an old lover; a pressed flower; a photograph; a punched ticket from Hampton Court Palace (for admission to State Apartments and Great Hall, The Great Kitchen and Cellars, The Tudor Tennis Court, and Banqueting House); even a toothless pocket comb. Having found the latter in a book she bought on the *quais* in Paris, Colette observed, "The human species never has sufficient shame when it comes to concealing the traces of its stopping places."

On the one hand, it is easy to agree with Colette. Reading a dog-eared book from the Boston Public Library is sometimes like sleeping in a stranger's unmade bed. On the other hand, what we have been taught in school and elsewhere tends to conceal, ignore, the human traces found inside books; it's as if these don't happen at all. But they do. What's more, not to recognize the book as a common stopping place for people is to overlook the fact people do not merely read books but live with them intensively in many different ways. Whether shared, loaned, borrowed, lost, bought, stolen, burned, received as either a gift or reward—or meted out as a punishment, books are not simply objects to be read but to be encountered as well.

The present collection seeks to, in a modest way, suggest what it is about books that makes them such special things, and in just what ways people live with them, regard them; why it is their readers and owners (the two are not always the same) can become so utterly fascinated with them. A wide range of material has been gathered here—from the great rescuer of books, Petrarch, to the brilliant American feminist writer, Margaret Fuller, to bookstall denizen Walter Jerrold—in the hopes of reflecting something of the diverse audiences books have attracted and held, as well as the multiple purposes which books have served.

Considerable effort, too, has been made to include work which reflects the viewpoint of the resolute reader as opposed to that of the zealous book collector; this stemming from the belief that the shared experience of a dedicated reader will connect more readily with most people's everyday book experiences. And, in so doing, reveal proportionately more about the subject.

While the majority of pieces in this book come from the pens of professional writers—hence professional readers, given the proximity between reading and writing—a few pieces hail from those readers whose employment lies outside the realm of letters. For their voices are essential to appreciating how books function in the everyday.

My major qualification for editing this collection about books is that I have been reading books randomly without any particular plan (one book always leads to another) every day for probably the past thirty years, usually at night and in bed. Does this make me an expert? No. Many friends have read as much or more, and in a much more disciplined way. Perhaps the only real distinction to be made is the fact I have maintained a ''Things Found in Books'' file, and other ones like it, for about the past seventeen years, ever since college. And left holding the ''file,'' so to speak, I have been asked to look into it, comment and share.

Reading over the pieces herein reminds me of a review William F. Buckley, Jr. wrote about the compact edition of the *Oxford English Dictionary*. As I recall, Mr. Buckley was ecstatic over at last obtaining his own copy of the *O.E.D.*, and in his enthusiasm for it set about installing alphabet tabs along each volume's fore-edge for ready reference. It is the only activity of Mr. Buckley's I have ever sympathized with or, for that matter, understood. Imagine someone of Mr. Buckley's stature, station, sticking on his own tabs to the 4,116 page 20 lb. *O.E.D.*! But such is the power of print, the attractiveness and usefulness of books.

This brings us back to the physical nature of books—which is, beyond all doubt, considerable. Mightily seductive, the book's many shapes and forms are historically rooted in such a broad array of earthy and, for the most part, common materials it is difficult to name them all, or even most. Clay. Skin. Bone. Stone. Metal. Wax. Grass. Leaves. Bark. Reeds. Cloth. Paper. They all have been used to make books with. And wood, too, of course, which accounts for the very origin of the word "book" itself ("boc" being Old English for "beech," a favorite inscribing surface for Germanic rune cutters). Whatever is available or handy has been, and continues to be, used for making books; in short, the shape and form of books are dictated by the world one inhabits and the materials found in one's own neighborhood. It needn't surprise us, then, when readers respond to books' physical qualities in strong fashion; these qualities resembling flesh and blood more than we may know.

But to move beyond the organic and inorganic chemistry of books and the fact that revelations of Allah to Muhammad were recorded on animal shoulder blades and tablets of white stone (among other materials), the majority of readers in this collection seem not to care a whit about how dashing, in any conventional sense, their books look so long as the books can be seen, held, smelt, read or otherwise appreciated.

"Thomson's Seasons . . . looks best (I maintain it) a little torn, and dogs-eared," writes Charles Lamb in "Detached Thoughts on Books and Reading." And even the flimsiest of books can be among the most memorable, influential, as Thomas Carter, an early nineteenth century tailor, testifies in his autobiography, *Memoirs of a Working Man* (1845). "I can remember all about them, their titles, their contents—and their external appearances. Some being without covers . . . farthing or half-penny histories of 'Tom Thumb,' 'Jack the Giant-killer,' 'Little Red Riding-hood,' and the like."

Perhaps, to take the cue from Thomas Carter, this is a good place to discuss the price of books. For historians of the book, this topic is as broad, rich and deep as the sea. For our own purposes, though, it can be simply stated that money figures in almost every piece in this collection. The marbelized mix of money and bookmaking has resulted over the years in numerous idiosyncratic, private, reader economies. Not only does the serious reader need money in order to eat but he needs money for the purchase of books as well. Solutions to the money problem, where it is a problem, are various and clever. But the availability of inexpensive editions, or of cheap used books, is cited over and over again by contributors here —from poet-journalist Leigh Hunt to novelist George Eliot to poet-journalist Bill Costley— as being of critical importance to the impassioned reader, who like George Gissing's Henry Ryecroft, may be no stranger to lean times.

The appearance in the nineteenth century of "the modern cheap and fertile press," to borrow Henry Thoreau's phrase from the "Reading" chapter in *Walden*, by no means meant books were automatically available in great and easily affordable numbers, or for free in libraries, to anyone with a passion for books. (Certainly not, for example, in England where literary historian Richard D. Altick's *The English Common Reader: A Social History of the Mass Reading Public 1800-1900* makes this point well.) Then, and even now, anyone addicted to books had to—has to—keep a weather eye out for not only inexpensive books but free, or affordable, library privileges; remainders; discards; browsing copies at the local bookseller's; and the well-stocked bookshelves of friends or benefactors, as well.

After its initial sale, a book exists in a hazy state of biblio-commerce and exchange which resists any kind of predictability, as a number of the following essays and excerpts suggest. Truly, if a book once it is sold does not fall into the realm of the Unknowable, then it certainly belongs in the realm of the Difficult-to-Trace, inasmuch as the publishing industry's distribution system may only control the whereabouts of an individual book for several weeks in the book's lifetime; then what happens—in reliable detail—is anybody's guess. A complex cultural and intellectual event of the first water.

Converting books into sacred objects, or regarding them as being precious, irreplaceable, a substitute for sunshine, are concepts that don't appear to sit well with some of our contributors. Thoreau, himself, unequivocally states, ''Decayed literature makes the richest of all soils,'' (Journal entry for 16 March 1852). Hazlitt, too, owns up in ''On Reading Old Books,'' that ''Books have in a great measure lost their power over me . . .'' Margaret Fuller advises in an extract from *Autobiographical Romance*, ''Children should not cull the fruits of reflection and observation early, but expand in the sun, and let thoughts come to them. They should not through books antedate their actual experiences . . .'' Even George Gissing's

10

Henry Ryecroft—certainly one of the most
remarkable portraits of a bibliophile in English
literature—unloads his cherished first edition
set of Gibbon (whose ''clean-paged quartos'' he,
originally, would have sold his coat for) when
his constant ''removals'' make it impractical for
him to keep it on.

Whatever it is that people notice about
books, it is never stated in casual or ordinary
terms, whether it be about the happy demolition
of a book through constant usage or the discovery of a cheap remainder which completes a set.
(How could it be otherwise? the hard-bitten
reader will ask.) Rest assured, the pieces that
follow do nothing to subtract from the state-
ment above. They determinedly approach (some
appearing, here, for the first time) books in
numerous insightful ways yet to be discussed in
this brief introduction. Books as gifts. Imaginary books. Books that do exist but aren't books.
Marginalia. Randy books. And, in a more
serious vein: Books in the battlefield. Books as
a tool of liberation from societal constraints and
inanities. Books as a weapon against slavery.

How does one arrange such a broad collection of insight, wit and wisdom within the tight
confines of a small book? Chronological, historical, thematical groupings all produced disap-
pointing results, largely, I suspect, because the
collection was not conceived with any one of

those determinants exclusively in mind. In truth, my idiosyncratic reading habits had more to do with the assembling of the collection than anything else. By arranging the pieces alphabetically, by author, I found that the old and the new, the lighthearted and the serious, and the known and the unknown, were blended together in a pleasing way—guaranteeing surprises and avoiding the unpleasantness of inappropriate formality. Just the ticket for a book entitled, *The Romance of the Book*.

—*MARSHALL BROOKS*
Spencer, Massachusetts

Books

By FAITH BALDWIN

I TRY TO KEEP MY LIBRARY down to four thousand by giving away a great many each year. As it is, books are all over the house, on tables, window seats, floors, even in the bathrooms. Current novels, masses of them and non-fiction and the strangest books bought for reference; strange only, I suppose as they elbow each other on the shelves, affording rather odd contrasts—radio and department stores, medical and airplanes, and a collection of books on Australia, Hawaii, Samoa, South America, and the far jungles.

Then there are shelves for English editions and for signed copies and for the books I collect. And the books I had as a child. I will discard several hundred modern novels a year but I won't discard the books which gave me such pleasure years ago. I have my tattered *Alice in Wonderland*, my *Wizard of Oz*, all the Nesbit books, and those of L. Allen Harker. I still possess my Andrew Lang's, my *Little Lame Prince*, my *Tapestry Room*. And somewhere on the shelves is a copy of Ouida's *Moths* which entranced me when I was fourteen, and one of Corelli's *Thelma*, which I thought was the most thrilling book ever written. I still have my Alcott's, and George Martin's *Emmy Lou* and the first edition I possessed of *The Wind in the Willows*. And what's more, I reread them.

Books have been meat and drink to me, they have been comfort and help, stimuli and narcotic. I'd rather read than eat!

I am sorry for people who don't like to read, yet perhaps they have escaped a long bondage—a bondage that started for me before I was six and has lasted forty years and will continue to enslave me until I die. There are some books which to me are more real than people. On my desk as I write is Naomi Mitchison's *Corn King and Spring Queen* which I reread every year, in order to lose myself in magic. On a shelf not too high is an edition of *Sherlock Holmes* I have had since childhood. For many years Mr. Holmes was my one hero, and when at thirteen I first met William Gillette, it was very hard to detach him from the stage Holmes' personality.

Books are the real magic casements. Even a bad book has something in it as a rule, an effort, a striving after expression. Books are both reality and escape. They shock us, sometimes, they stun us, they trouble us—but always they delight us. They sharpen our insight, set our imaginations free. And they are always the

BALDWIN

least expensive and most valuable form of entertainment as well as education.

And, confidentially, I'd much rather read than write them.

—1939

Books Within Books

By *MAX BEERBOHM*

THEY MUST, I SUPPOSE, be classed among *biblia abiblia*. Ignored in the catalogue of any library, not one of them lurking in any uttermost cavern under the reading-room of the British Museum, none of them ever printed even for private circulation, these books written by this and that character in fiction are books only by courtesy and good will.

But how few, after all, the books that *are* books! Charles Lamb let his kind heart master him when he made that too brief list of books that *aren't*. Book is an honourable title, not to be conferred lightly. A volume is not necessarily, as Lamb would have had us think, a book because it can be read without difficulty. The test is, whether is was worth reading. Had the author something to set forth? And had he the specific gift for setting it forth in written words? And did he use this rather rare gift conscientiously and to the full? And were his words well and appropriately printed and bound? If you can say Yes to these questions, then only, I submit, is the title of "book" deserved. If Lamb were alive now, he certainly would draw the line

closer than he did. Published volumes were few
in his day (though not, of course, few enough).
Even he, in all the plenitude of his indulgence,
would now have to demur that at least 90 per
cent of the volumes that the publishers thrust on
us, so hectically, every spring and autumn, are
abiblia.

What would he have to say of the novels,
for example? These commodities are all very
well in their way, no doubt. But let us have no
illusions as to what their way is. The poulterer
who sells strings of sausages does not pretend
that every individual sausage is in itself remarkable. He does not assure us that "this is a
sausage that gives furiously to think," or "this
is a singularly beautiful and human sausage,"
or "this is undoubtedly the sausage of the year."
Why are such distinctions drawn by the publisher? When he publishes, as he sometimes does, a
novel that is a book (or at any rate would be a
book if it were decently printed and bound)
then by all means let him proclaim its difference
—even at the risk of scaring away the majority
of readers.

I admit that I myself might be found in
that majority. I am shy of masterpieces; nor is
this merely because of the many times I have
been disappointed at not finding anything at all
like what the publishers expected me to find. As
a matter of fact, those disappointments are dim

in my memory: it is long since I ceased to take publishers' opinions as my guide. I trust now, for what I ought to read, to the advice of a few highly literary friends. But so soon as I am told that I "must" read this or that, and have replied that I instantly will, I become strangely loth to do anything of the sort. And what I like about books within books is that they never can prick my conscience. It is extraordinarily comfortable that they don't exist.

And yet—for, even as Must implants distaste, so does Can't stir sweet longings—how eagerly would I devour these books within books! What fun, what a queer emotion, to fish out from a fourpenny-box; in a windy by-street, *Walter Lorraine*, by Arthur Pendennis, or *Passion Flowers*, by Rosa Bunion! I suppose poor Rosa's muse, so fair and so fervid in Rosa's day, would seem a trifle fatigued now; but what allowances one would make! Lord Steyne said of *Walter Lorraine* that it was "very clever and wicked." I fancy we should apply neither epithet now. Indeed, I have always suspected that Pen's maiden effort may have been on a plane with *The Great Hoġarty Diamond*. Yet I vow would I not skip a line of it.

Who Put Back the Clock? is another work which I especially covet. Poor Gideon Forsyth! He was abominably treated, as Stevenson relates, in the matter of that grand but grisly piano; and I have always hoped that perhaps, in the end, as a sort of recompense, Fate ordained that the novel he had anonymously written should be rescued from oblivion and found by discerning critics to be not at all bad. Such an humiliation as Gideon's is the more poignant to me because it is so rare in English fiction. In nine cases out of ten, a book within a book is an immediate, an immense success.

On the whole, our novelists have always tended to optimism—especially they who have written mainly to please their public. It pleases the public to read about any sort of success. The greater, the more sudden and violent the success, the more valuable is it as ingredient in a novel. And, since the average novelist lives always in a dream that one of his works will somehow "catch on" as no other work ever has caught on yet, it is very natural that he should fondly try meanwhile to get this dream realised for him, vicariously, by this or that creature of his fancy. True, he is usually too self-conscious to let this creature achieve his sudden fame and endless fortune through a novel. Usually it is a play that does the trick. In the Victorian time it was almost always a book of poems. Oh for the spacious days of Tennyson and Swinburne! In how many a three-volume novel is mentioned some "slim octavo," which seems, from the account given, to have been as arresting as

Poems and Ballads without being less accept-
able than *Idylls of the King!* These verses
were always the anonymous work of some very
young, very poor man, who supposed they had
fallen still-born from the press until one day, a
week or so after publication, as he walked
"moodily" and "in a brown study" along the
Strand, having given up all hope now that he
would ever be in a position to ask Hilda to be
his wife, a friend accosted him—"Seen 'The
Thunderer' this morning? By George, there's a
column review of a new book of poems," etc. In
some three-volume novel that I once read at a
seaside place, having borrowed it from the little
circulating library, there was a young poet
whose sudden leap into the front rank has
always laid a special hold on my imagination.
The name of the novel itself I cannot recall; but
I remember the name of the young poet—Aylmer
Deane; and the forever unforgettable title of his
book of verse was *Poments: Being Poems of
the Mood and the Moment.* What would I not
give to possess a copy of that work?

Though he had suffered, and though suffering
is a sovereign preparation for great work, I did
not at the onset foresee that Aylmer Deane was
destined to wear the laurel. In real life I have
rather a *flair* for future eminence. In novels I
am apt to be wise only after the event. There
the young men who do in due course take the

town by storm have seldom shown (to my dull eyes) promise. Their spoken thoughts have seemed to me no more profound or pungent than my own. All that is best in these authors goes into their work. But, though I complain of them on this count, I admit that the thrill for me of their triumphs is the more rapturous because every time it catches me unawares. One of the greatest emotions I ever had was from the triumph of *The Gift of Gifts*. Of this novel within a novel the author was not a young man at all, but an elderly clergyman whose life had been spent in a little rural parish. He was a dear, simple old man, a widower. He had a large family, a small stipend. Judge, then, of his horror when he found that his eldest son, "a scholar at Christminster College, Oxbridge," had run into debt for many hundreds of pounds. Where to turn? The father was too proud to borrow of the neighbourly nobleman who in Oxbridge days had been his "chum." Nor had the father ever practised the art of writing. (We are told that "his sermons were always ex-*tempore*.") But, years ago, "he had once thought of writing a novel based on an experi-ence which happened to a friend of his." This novel, in the fullness of time, he now proceeded to write, though "without much hope of suc-cess." He knew that he was suffering from heart-disease. But he worked "feverishly, night after night," we are told, "in his old faded dressing-gown, till the dawn mingled with the light of his candle and warned him to snatch a few hours' rest, failing which he would be little able to perform the round of parish duties that awaited him in the daytime." No wonder he had "not much hope." No wonder I had no spark of hope for him. But what are obstacles for but to be overleapt? What avails heart-disease, what avail eld and feverish haste and total lack of literary training, as against the romantic instinct of the lady who created the Rev. Charles Hailing? *"The Gift of Gifts* was acclaimed as a masterpiece by all the first-class critics." Also, it very soon "brought in" ten times as much money as was needed to pay off the debts of its author's eldest son. Nor, though Charles Hailing died some months later, are we told that he died from the strain of com-position. We are left merely to rejoice at know-ing he knew at the last "that his whole family was provided for."

I wonder why it is that, whilst these Charles Hailings and Aylmer Deanes delightfully abound in the lower reaches of English fiction, we have so seldom found in the work of our great novelists anything at all about the writing of a great book. It is true, of course, that our great novelists have never had for the idea of literature itself that passion which has always

burned in the great French ones. Their own art
has never seemed to them the most important
and interesting thing in life. Also it is true that
they have had other occupations—fox-hunting,
preaching, editing magazines, what not. Yet to
them literature must, as their own main task,
have had a peculiar interest and importance.
No fine work can be done without concentration
and self-sacrifice and toil and doubt. It is nonsense to imagine that our great novelists have
just forged ahead or ambled along, reaching
their goal, in the good old English fashion, by
sheer divination of the way to it. A fine book,
with all that goes to the making of it, is as fine
a theme as a novelist can have. But it is a part
of English hypocrisy—or, let it be more politely
said, English reserve—that, whilst we are fluent
enough in grumbling about small inconveniences,
we insist on making light of any great difficulties
or griefs that may beset us. And just there, I
suppose, is the reason why our great novelists
have shunned great books as subject-matter. It
is fortunate for us (jarring though it is to our
patriotic sense) that Mr. Henry James was not
born an Englishman, that he was born of a race
of specialists—men who are impenitent specialists in whatever they take up, be it sport,
commerce, politics, anything. And it is fortunate
for us that in Paris, and in the straitest literary
sect there, his method began to form itself, and

the art of prose fiction became to him a religion.
In that art he finds as much inspiration as Swinburne found in the art of poetry. Just as Swinburne was the most learned of our poets, so is
Mr. James the most learned of our—let us say
"our"—prose-writers. I doubt whether the
heaped total of his admirations would be found
to outweigh the least one of the admirations
that Swinburne had. But, though he has been a
level-headed reader of the works that are good
enough for him to praise, his abstract passion
for the art of fiction itself has always been fierce
and constant. Partly to the Parisian, partly to
the American element in him we owe the stories
that he, and of "our" great writers he only,
has written about books and the writers of
books.

Here, indeed, in these incomparable stories,
are imaginary great books that are as real to us
as real ones are. Sometimes, as *The Author of
"Beltraffio,"* a great book itself is the very
hero of the story. (We are not told what exactly
was the title of that second book which Ambi-
ent's wife so hated that she let her child die
rather than that he should grow up under the
influence of its author; but I have a queer conviction that it was *The Daisies.*) Usually, in
these stories, it is through the medium of some
ardent young disciple, speaking in the first person, that we become familiar with the great

writer. It is thus that we know Hugh Vereker, throughout whose twenty volumes was woven that message, or meaning, that "figure in the carpet," which eluded even the elect. It is thus that we know Neil Paraday, the MS. of whose last book was mislaid and lost so tragically, so comically. And it is also through Paraday's disciple that we make incidental acquaintance with Guy Walsingham, the young lady who wrote *Obsessions*, and with Dora Forbes, the burly man with a red moustache, who wrote *The Other Way Round*. These two books are the only inferior books mentioned by Mr. James. But stay, I was forgetting *The Top of the Tree*, by Amy Evans; and also those nearly forty volumes by Henry St. George. For all the greatness of his success in life, Henry St. George is the saddest of the authors portrayed by Mr. James. His *Shadowmere* was splendid, and its splendour is the measure of his shame—the shame he bore so bravely—in the ruck of his "output." He is the only one of those authors who did not do his best. Of him alone it may not be said that he was "generous and delicate and pursued the prize." He is a more pathetic figure than even Dencombe, the author of *The Middle Years*. Dencombe's grievance was against fate, not against himself. The scene of Dencombe's death is one of the most deeply-beautiful things ever done by Mr. James. It is so beautiful as to be hardly sad; it rises and glows and gladdens. It is more exquisite than anything in *The Middle Years*. No, I will not say that. Mr. James's art can always carry to us the conviction that his characters' books are as fine as his own.

I crave—it may be a foolish whim, but I do crave—ocular evidence for my belief that those books were written and were published. I want to see them all ranged along goodly shelves. A few days ago I sat in one of those libraries which seem to be doorless. Nowhere, to the eye, was broken the array of serried volumes. Each door was flush with the surrounding shelves; across each the edges of the shelves were mimicked and in the spaces between these edges the backs of books were pasted congruously with the whole effect. Some of these backs had been taken from actual books, others had been made specially and were stamped with facetious titles that rather depressed me. "Here," thought I, "are the shelves on which Dencombe's works ought to be made manifest. And Neil Paraday's too, and Vereker's." Not Henry St. George's, of course: he would not himself have wished it, poor fellow! I would have nothing of his except *Shadow-mere*. But Ray Limbert!—I would have all of his, including a first edition of *The Major Key*, "that fiery-hearted rose as to which we watched in private the formation of petal after petal, and flame after flame"; and also *The Hidden Heart*, "the shortest of his novels, but perhaps the loveliest," as Mr. James and I have always thought. . . . How my fingers would hover along these shelves, always just going to alight, but never, lest the spell were broken, alighting!

How well they would look there, those treasures of mine! And, most of them having been issued in the seemly old three-volume form, how many shelves they would fill! But I should find a place certainly for a certain small brown book adorned with a gilt griffin between wheat-sheaves, *The Pilgrim's Scrip*, that delightful though anonymous work of my old friend Austin Absworthy Bearne Feverel. And I should like to find a place for *Poems*, by Aurora Leigh. Mr. Snodgrass's book of verses might grace one of the lower shelves. (What is the title of it? *Amelia's Bower*, I hazard.) *Recollections of the Late Lord Byron and Others*, by Captain Sumph, would be somewhere; for Sumph did, you will be glad to hear, take Shandon's advice and compile a volume. Bungay published it. Indeed, of the books for which I should find room there are a good few that bear the imprimatur of Bungay. *Desperation, or The Fugitive Duchess*, by The Hon. Percy Popjoy, was Bungay's; and so, of course, were *Passion Flowers* and *Walter Lorraine*. Of the books issued by the rival firm of Bacon I possess but one: *Memoirs of the Poisoners*, by Dr.

Slocum. Near to Popjoy's romance would be *The Lady Flabella*, of which Mrs. Wititterly said to Kate Nickleby, "So voluptuous, is it not —so soft?" *Who Put Back the Clock?* would have a place of honour (unearned by its own merits?). Among other novels that I could not spare, *The Gift of Gifts* would conspicuously gleam. As for *Poments*—ah, I should not be content with one copy of that. Even at the risk of crowding out a host of treasures, I vow I would have a copy of every one of the editions that *Poments* ran through.

—1914

Memoirs of a Working Man

By *THOMAS CARTER*

MY FAVOURITE AMUSEMENTS were reading, gardening, and walking in the adjacent fields and meadows. Of these, however, reading was my chief delight; for I could avail myself of this the most easily and regularly. I willingly left every other pastime for the sake of a book that suited my taste. And I valued this pleasure the more, because it was only at leisure times that I was permitted to enjoy it. I had not much time at my own disposal, being usually employed in one or other of the ways I have already stated. If it were at knitting, I was forbidden to read until I had finished my allotted task. Sometimes when I tried to evade this law, I was detected, and severely reprimanded by my mother, whose maxim was, that two distinct things could not both be well done at the same time. At other times I succeeded in gratifying my wishes by getting into some secluded place, where I could avoid observation. In order that I might the better escape detection, I took pains to get through my task in due time, and, moreover, was careful to do it well. In these efforts I was generally successful, for, on making the experiment, I found it possible to knit—both quickly and neatly—without having much occasion to look at my work. In this way I beguiled many a tedious hour at the time I am now referring to, and also during several years following, towards the close of which I thus contrived to read 'Robinson Crusoe,' and a brief 'History of England,' with some other books whose titles I do not now remember. The books that first fell in my way, besides those that belonged to my parents, were few, and of little worth. At that time the stock of books within the reach of poor children was very small, while the price of such as were useful was generally higher than poor people could afford. There were then no cheap well-printed neatly bound books on subjects at once instructive and amusing, such as are now so abundantly supplied by benevolent societies and enterprising publishers. The once general prejudice against educating the poor was then very prevalent, while many of the poor had no wish to be taught. Moreover, the books that were given to them were generally printed badly, and done up in unsightly covers; while their contents were seldom much more attractive than was their external appearance. It did not in those days seem to be understood that abstract treatises on religious or other serious subjects were not adapted to fix the attention of children and other young persons. There was

but little recognition of the obvious fact that
the human mind needs recreation as well as
instruction; that it desires amusement, and,
therefore, will seek to obtain it from frivolous,
if not dangerous sources, in the absence of such
as are useful and innocent. . . .

I have now—after an interval of more than
forty-five years—a clear recollection of the
little books which I read when a child, and
which then formed the principal part of a poor
child's "Entertaining Library." I can remember
all about them, their titles, their contents—and
their external appearance. Some, being without
covers, were sold for the price indicated in the
following laudatory stanza, with which, and a
suitable vignette, the title-page of one was
embellished:

> "A very pretty thing
> For daddy's darling;
> Tom Thumb and the piper
> And all for a farthing."

Others were of higher pretensions and prouder
aspect, being enclosed in gay covers of party-
coloured or gilded paper, and therefore were
sold at the comparatively large price of a half-
penny.

It may seem to be little better than trifling
to write about farthing or halfpenny histories
of 'Tom Thumb,' 'Jack the Giant-killer,' 'Little

Red Riding-hood,' and the like; but when it is considered that the human mind generally retains, in mature years, much of the tastes and habits it acquired in childhood, it will not be difficult to believe that important consequences may and often do arise out of circumstances or practices which in themselves are of little worth or moment.

From much observation, I am led to think that the preference shown by many persons for such books as treat of wholly fictitious or merely frivolous subjects, to the utter neglect of all such as are instructive and important, is in a great degree owing to their having been, while children, accustomed to read very little besides fabulous and foolish tales. That this perverted or false taste has an injurious bearing upon their habits and condition, is, I think, too evident to need any laboured proof. In my own case, such books as these did me but little harm, inasmuch as my prevailing desire was to obtain some useful knowledge; consequently I was soon satiated with what was adapted only to please a vagrant or a sickly fancy. When I first began to read for amusement, I had, as has been hinted, access to but few books that were likely to be useful as well as entertaining. My parent's stock consisted of two Bibles, a Common Prayer Book, a Universal 'Spelling-book,' Watts's 'Divine and Moral Songs,' with some tattered and odd volumes of sermons and other theological disquisitions. Among the latter of these was nearly the whole of a huge folio volume, which was then as much beyond my power to handle conveniently as its contents were above my comprehension; yet, in the absence of more attractive compositions, I sometimes read considerable portions of even this giant-sized and uninviting volume. But my attention was chiefly given to the historical and poetical parts of the Bible; these I read with great interest, but mingled of course with much childish wonder and misapprehension. How much I needed the aid of a competent teacher will be manifest when I state that, for a long time, I believed the books of "the Kings" and of "the Chronicles" to be unconnected narratives of two distinct series of events; and also, that the four Gospels were consecutive portions of the history of Jesus Christ, so that I supposed there had been four crucifixions, four resurrections, and the like. I was, indeed, sometimes perplexed by the apparently repeated occurrence of events so nearly resembling each other; nor could I perceive the exact design or bearing of these events; but I knew no one of whom I could ask for the needed explanations. . . .

In general I could easily get through my afternoon's work in less than an hour, while the usual time for being in the schoolroom was three

hours. I thus had full two hours of spare time,
which I continued to spend very pleasantly, and
perhaps usefully: my main object was indeed
amusement, but the recreation I chose was, I
think, instructive also; this was reading, for
which I had now greater facilities than formerly.
I borrowed such books as I could from my schoolfellows, but sometimes found this to be an unsat-
isfactory plan: on one occasion I wished to read
a book, which, however, the owner would not let
me have without a pecuniary consideration; I
therefore hired it for a stipulated time, but
shortly after I had paid him, which was at the
time of hiring, he reclaimed it, and refused to
return the money: I was indignant at his injus-
tice, but there was no remedy, for he was strong
enough to enforce the law of "might" against
that of "right," and therefore I quietly submit-
ted, although I was sorely grieved at being
hindered from using 'The Looking-glass for the
Mind,' and the more so because I had hired the
book at the expense of all my cash, amounting
to no less a sum than three halfpence.

This incident taught me to be more circum-
spect in making bargains with schoolfellows, by
none of whom was I afterwards thus defrauded,
either of pence or pleasure. . . .

—1845

Looking Backwards

By *COLETTE*

IKE FLIES ON HONEY they hasten, cluster, feed. . . . The comparison is not new but is inevitable. Everything suggests it: the noonday hour, the splendour of these autumn days, the haste and assiduity of these open-air readers.

Their meeting-place is old, beautiful and respected. The rarity of passers-by exposes to view and aerates this square, which gives access to a famous theatre, a garden, a palace, which were royal once.

The Louvre and its flowerbeds, Rivoli and its arcades, the Bourse and the Bank release at noon a small wave, a crowd of toilers who take their repast and their recreation in less than two hours. It seems plain to me that they are concerned more nowadays than formerly with the one, to the detriment of the other. In the avenue de l'Opera a second bookshop receives the same devotions and I am assured that the treacherous draughts beneath the Odeon discourage none of those absorbed in reading. But here, in my neighbourhood, which is also that of the Theatre-Francais, the honey-trap, the book, bursts its bounds and spills over, offers itself to

eager hands and eyes. The ancient atlas, with
its copper-plate engravings where Aeolus puffs
the islands and dolphins sport between two
continents, oppresses Giraudoux and Victor
Cherbuliez with its due weight. The 'bargain
book', old before its time, hot and peeling, its
stitching hanging out at the back, belongs to
you, to me, to everyone. But leave it, as I do,
to those who will not buy it, who read fifty
pages today, as many tomorrow, the end of the
volume the day after. . . .

They are recognizable. Young for the most
part, they read standing up and, standing, they
rest with one leg over the other. Bare-headed,
boys and girls, they haven't yet any overcoat or
three-quarter jacket; perhaps they'll be without
one right through the winter. . . . For the
moment they're not in need since, with the
autumn, the sun gradually moves south and
touches their shoulder and, above all, they hold
an open book. The handy outdoor display serv-
ing as a desk, they turn the pages and keep one
hand free because they lunch while reading. I
should much rather—so great is our cowardice,
our desire to avoid what wounds us—I should
much rather not know what it is they lunch on,
so hastily, so meagrely. They too, proud as they
are, prefer us not to know that, for instance, the
large cream-horn they put to their mouths is a
loaf which may or may not be stuffed with meat,

disguised in a bundle of papers. There is also
the meal hidden in a pocket, in a handbag, from
which one detaches little mouthfuls between two
fingers, as if absentmindedly. . . .

Standlng, absorbed in its dream, part of
Parisian youth reads passionately. It has always
read at the bookstalls and along the *quais*,
imprisoned under the stall-roofs like a sparrow
in a trap. But I believe that it did so in former
times with less ardour and application. I'm the
more sure of this from an attentive reading of
the letters I get from strangers.

'Madame Colette, I would like some books,
how can one exchange books? We have a varied
enough little collection—travel, novels, natural
science—read and reread, and it's hardly possible
to buy new books just now. . . . Madame, why
aren't there more reading-rooms? . . .'

I shall be told that the young people of both
sexes, eager to read—that is to say, roused by a
painful aspiration, a need to fly in spirit towards
a mental illumination, to forsake their daily
tasks—are engaged in reading, precisely, 'no
matter what'. Agreed. I tell myself as much.
Where is the harm? They read and contemplate
entomological works, odd instalments of books
on art, a fine old novel by Alphonse Daudet,
incomplete runs of medical journals, manuals of
practical science, a stout legal tome, the diary
of an eighteenth-century traveller, a miracle of

slowness, naivety and fond curiousity. They leaf through a marvellous *Paris ancien*, raise their eyes and, astonished, recognize it all around them. They make contact with a past which they renounced from ignorance, a capital where they were born but which they do not even look at; they are moved by the thought that it might have perished without their having ever truly loved it. . . .

So let them read no matter what. That's what I did in my youth, given the run of a library where everything was grist to my mill and where nothing would have been considered suitable for me at six, at ten, at fourteen. . . . Forbidden books, over-serious books and too frivolous books as well, boring books, dazzling books which shine out at random and close their temple doors behind the entranced child. . . . The very randomness of reading is noble. Every book, initially ill-absorbed, is a conquest. Its jungle of ideas and words will open out, one day, on to a calm and friendly landscape.

—1942

The Life of Thomas Cooper

By *THOMAS COOPER*

JOHN HOUGH, MY NEW FRIEND, had been brought up as a dissenter; and he had very decided views and opinions on nonconformity and dissent. . . . He was, however, a broad general reader, had an excellent library, and made me welcome to the loan of every book in it that I desired to read.

I had come to the knowledge that there was another great supply of old English literature which I could make use of. "Nathaniel Robinson, mercer," many years before, had left his library for the use of the inhabitants of the town; but it had been thrust aside into a corner, and almost forgotten. I was in ecstasies to find the dusty, cobwebbed shelves loaded with Hooker, and Bacon, and Cudworth, and Stillingfleet, and Locke, and Jeremy Taylor, and Tillotson, and Bates, and Bishop Hall, and Samuel Clarke, and Warburton, and Bull, and Waterland, and Bentley, and Bayle, and Ray, and Derham, and a score of other philosophers and divines,—mingled with Stanley's "History of Philosophers," and its large full-length portraits —Ogilvy's "Embassies to Japan and China," with their large curious engravings—Speed's and

Rapin's folio histories of England—Collier's
"Church History"—Fuller's "Holy War"—
Foxe's "Book of Martyrs," the first edition, in
black letter, and with its odd, rude plates—and
countless other curiosities and valuables.

I must mention another little piece of good
fortune that now befell me—although I was
indebted for it partly to real kindness, and
partly to a little roguery. The dear old lady,
Mrs. Trevor, of whom I had purchased my lead
pencils and water colours when a child, and
from whose tattered and worn Circulating
Library I had borrowed so many volumes of
tales, novels, and romances, always regarded me
as a kind of pet; and I was still her customer for
papers and pens, and so on. I noted that a few
of the gentry had commenced a "Book Society"
at her shop. The subscription of two guineas per
annum was above my power to pay; but, as I
took the liberty, one day, to handle some of the
new volumes and periodicals, she closed the shop
door, and, coming close to me, whispered that
she thought she could accommodate me with the
loan of the books. Suppose I gave her ten shillings for the books of each season, and took care
to fetch them in the evening, about the time
that shops closed, when it would be certain that
none of the genteel subscribers would be in the
way?

So the forbidden fruit was secured once

more; and I went home all in a glow with delight
—for I was taking two numbers of the ''London
Magazine'' with me, and the first volume of
Scott's ''Kenilworth''!

. . . My historical reading was a great delight. I read, thoroughly, Gibbon's ''Decline and
Fall,'' and followed it up by reading the Prelim-
inary Discourse to Sale's translation of the
Koran, and a translation of Mosheim's Church
History. I made written notes, often, as I went
along. I analysed Dr. Clarke's ''Demonstrations
of the Being and Attributes,'' and it was done
so completely that I seemed to know the book
by heart. My friend Hough approved it greatly,
and showed it to others, till—at last—it was
begged, and given away to one who was prepar-
ing for the Christian ministry.

In the hurry and whirl of my changeful life,
I have lost the journal that I kept so strictly in
those years, and all written records of my reading; but I can recall the feeling of pleasure, or
profound interest, I experienced in reading many
a volume; and the feeling is often associated
with some feature of a landscape, or turn of the
woods, or appearance of the hills or lanes where
I walked. Thus the dear old remembrances often
flash upon me, after all these years; and I seem
to see the page, and the rural spot where I read
it, as clearly as if it had happened only an hour
ago. How strange it seems—seeing that I, often,

cannot call to mind whether I wrote to such a person last week; and, most commonly, forget the names and features of persons with whom I have but lately become acquainted,—nay, often forget, utterly, some things I saw, or some actions I performed, not a month ago!

Blair's "Lectures on Rhetoric and the Belles Lettres" was another book that I analysed very closely and laboriously, being determined on acquiring a thorough judgment of style and literary excellence. All this practice seemed to destroy the desire of composing poetry of my own. Milton's verse seemed to overawe me, as I committed it to memory, and repeated it daily; and the perfection of his music, as well as the gigantic stature of his intellect, were fully perceived by my mind. The wondrous knowledge of the heart unfolded by Shakspeare, made me shrink into insignificance; while the sweetness, the marvellous power of expression and grandeur of his poetry seemed to transport me, at times, out of the vulgar world of circumstances in which I lived bodily. Besides the two great poets, I made myself familiar with others; and committed to memory thousands of lines by Burns, and Coleridge, and Wordsworth, and Scott, and Byron, and Moore, and Campbell, and Southey, and Keats. And the repetition, daily, of poetry displaying all the harmonies of rhythm—all the opulence of the stores of ex-

pressing thought—repressed all desire of composing poetry myself. I said to myself, daily—
"I am educating my ear and my mind, and I
shall be ripe for my true work in time."

The culture I attempted for myself was
broad enough, at any rate—for I often diverged
into miscellaneous reading, and can remember
the pleasure with which I went through the elder
Disraeli's "Curiosities of Literature," "Calami-
ties of Authors," and "Quarrels of Authors,"
Warton's "History of Early English Poetry,"
Johnson's "Lives of the Poets," "Rasselas,"
etc., Boswell's "Life of Johnson," Landor's
"Imaginary Conversations," Southey's "Book
of the Church," Lingard's "Anglo-Saxon
Antiquities," Colton's "Lacon," Douglas of
Cavers on the "Advancement of Society,"
Bullock's "Mexico," Richardson's "Travels in
Egypt and the Holy Land," Head's "Rough
Notes of a Journey to the Andes," and many
other volumes of travels.

The novels of Scott I took care to have from
the shelves of the dear old lady's shop, as early
after their first appearance as I could come by
them,—while I also indulged myself occasionally
by reading the new pages of Washington Irving,
or such novels as Mrs. Shelley's thrilling creation of "Frankenstein," and Lockhart's sterling
stories of "Valerius" and "Reginald Dalton."

The later poetry of Byron, contained in

"The Liberal," and that published separately,
with the new volumes of Campbell, Moore,
Milman, and others, I had also, *by favour*, from
those kindly shelves in the little shop I had
frequented from a child. . . .

—1872

I Always Keep Jeffers Around

By BILL COSTLEY

IT'S IMPOLITIC TO ADMIT a lifelong attachment to anyone but Walt Whitman in 1992 (his death centenary) but Walt wasn't my main man after 1959—the year I read aloud the opening lines of "By Blue Ontario's Shore" in the King's Rook Coffeehouse in downtown Marblehead, Massachusetts, as my first spontaneous poetry reading, amazing my best friend, John Broderick, speechless beside me in the empty coffeehouse one Saturday afternoon. We were seventeen and it was pre-Vietnam.

Our literary antidote to Robert Frost and official literature was the Beats, who were suddenly and amazingly available in a Dell paperback anthology—*The Beat Generation and the Angry Young Men*—we'd found on a drugstore rack. Ginsberg's "Howl" was carefully sanitized there, but we got the obvious points despite the asterisks.

"Blue Ontario" was my first and last reading of Whitman. Ever since, I've kept Robinson Jeffers around instead—after seeing a few lines of his under a photograph of a shattering image of sunlight in a *Life* magazine spread on Ameri-

can poets. The lines were from his ''Apology for
Bad Dreams'':

> He brays humanity in a mortar to bring
> the savor
> From the bruised root: a man having bad
> dreams, who
> invents victims, is only the ape of that
> God.
> He washes it out with tears and many
> waters, calcines it
> with fire in the red crucible,
> Deforms it, makes it horrible to itself:
> the spirit flies out
> and stands naked, he sees the spirit,
> He takes it in the naked ecstasy, it breaks
> in his hand,
> the atom is broken. . .

This was the first conscious post Atom
Bomb poetry I had ever seen, written the way
Whitman might have if he were living in the
1950s and not the 1850s. I found the rest of the
poem in a badly worn, Scotch-taped second
hand Penguin Signet (first edition, 1948) of
Selden Rodman's *100 American Poems* at
Eddie's Junk Shop in Lynn, Massachusetts'
'Brickyard' ghetto, around the corner from the
New York Model (Jewish) Bakery where my
father and I bought Danish pastry and bulkies
Sunday mornings after Mass. Eddie charged

five cents for all of his used books, most with their covers still intact. My life was forever changed by finding *The Pocket Reader* (1941) with Archibald MacLeish's verse play for radio, "The Fall of the City" (which I soon imitated in my first play, written for my English lit. course at St. John's Prep. School) and also Kressman Taylor's unforgettable epistolary novella, *Address at Unbekannt*, which drew my mind thru a dark extruding mask like wire.

At Eddie's I also found Saul Bellow's *Seize the Day* in the Dell paperback edition with "The Gonzaga Manuscript" in it (Bellow's parody of Henry James' *The Aspern Papers*) and a one-act play, "The Wrecker" about a couple's apartment on the last day of their building's being urban-renewed by the wrecker's ball. I also found a discarded copy of Ray Bradbury's *Farenheit 451* with four short stories in it (including "The Swing"). For me, in 1959, Eddie's was what the Lynn Public Library had been for Lynn's leading literary figure then, novelist Truman Nelson.

I still keep that paperback edition of Rodman's *100 American Poems* (and copies of it) on one shelf of a red bookcase in the back room with all my Jeffers books—because I always need him there (and all the other poets in it, particularly Kenneth Fearing, whom I later learned to appreciate in my late thirties and read aloud in public; he replaced Whitman for me, too).

Falling for Jeffers at seventeen clearly illustrated my profound post-WW2 disenchantment with the optimistic America Whitman stood for and stands for still. Well before WW2, Jeffers was America's Negative Whitman—what Whitman saw opening, Jeffers saw closing. As America's most expansive poet of negative conscience, Jeffers despised American Imperialism—WW1, WW2, The Bomb, Korea. He died in 1962, just barely before JFK got us into Vietnam.

Resisting conscription for Vietnam soon changed my life even more than the books I found at Eddie's, but they'd prepared me for it. Seriously disaffected by the time I went into the Lynn draft board at eighteen to register, I forewarned them I was going to be a Conscientious Objector when I was called up. They were visbily astonished: "You're a Roman Catholic! Only Jehovah's Witnesses refuse induction." Well, this was one Roman Catholic who had read Jeffers and Fearing the year before and he was definitely not gonna go.

Even now, other Jeffers books are on a shelf in that red bookcase behind me as I write this: some early editions in the black-backed, Liveright bindings; his collected letters, ordered in 1972 ($10.95) from a *New York Times Book*

Review ad; a few books of homage (for the color photos)—jumbled behind me as I write this on a Philips (NL) Vendex Head Start System Turbo 888-XT (amber monitor) in WordPerfect (4.1).

It's now two-and-a-half conscientious decades, pre- and post-Vietnam, away from Jeffers' pencils and tower in Big Sur where he read Sir Walter Scott novels to his young sons Donnan and Garth who would subdivide that plot of land into small parcels leaving just the tower standing on one of them.

Jeffers might well have seen it coming. He certainly predicted America's "... heavily thickening to Empire" in "Shine, Perishing Republic (1925)"—"Shine, Republic (1934)"—"We Are Those People" (1948); bitter, ironic short poems warning us what America has really made of itself in the twentieth century. For that, Whitman was absolutely no help at all.

—1993

The Life & Times of Douglass

By FREDERICK DOUGLASS

WHEN I WAS ABOUT thirteen years old, and had succeeded in learning to read, every increase of knowledge, especially respecting the Free States, added something to the almost intolerable burden of the thought—"I am a slave for life." To my bondage I saw no end. It was a terrible reality, and I shall never be able to tell how sadly that thought chafed my young spirit. Fortunately, or unfortunately, about this time in my life, I had made enough money to buy what was then a very popular school book, viz: the *Columbian Orator*. I bought this addition to my library, of Mr. Knight, on Thames street, Fell's Point, Baltimore, and paid him fifty cents for it. I was first led to buy this book, by hearing some little boys say they were going to learn some little pieces out of it for the Exhibition. This volume was, indeed, a rich treasure, and every opportunity afforded me, for a time, was spent in diligently perusing it. Among much other interesting matter, that which I had perused and reperused with unflagging satisfaction, was a short dialogue between a master and his slave. The slave is represented as having been recaptured, in a second attempt to run away; and the master opens the dialogue with an upbraiding speech, charging the slave with ingratitude, and demanding to know what he has to say in his own defense. Thus upbraided, and thus called upon to reply, the slave rejoins, that he knows how little anything that he can say will avail, seeing that he is completely in the hands of his owner; and with noble resolution, calmly says, "I submit to my fate." Touched by the slave's answer, the master insists upon his further speaking, and recapitulates the many acts of kindness which he has performed toward the slave, and tells him he is permitted to speak for himself. Thus invited to the debate, the quondam slave made a spirited defense of himself, and thereafter the whole argument, for and against slavery, was brought out. The master was vanquished at every turn in the argument; and seeing himself to be thus vanquished, he generously and meekly emancipates the slave, with his best wishes for his prosperity. It is scarcely necessary to say, that a dialogue, with such an origin, and such an ending—read when the fact of my being a slave was a constant burden of grief—powerfully affected me; and I could not help feeling that the day might come, when the well-directed answers made by the slave to the master, in this instance, would find their counterpart in myself.

This, however, was not all the fanaticism which I found in this *Columbian Orator*. I met there one of Sheridan's mighty speeches, on the subject of Catholic Emancipation, Lord Chatham's speech on the American war, and speeches by the great William Pitt and by Fox. These were all choice documents to me, and I read them, over and over again, with an interest that was ever increasing, because it was ever gaining in intelligence; for the more I read them, the better I understood them. The reading of these speeches added much to my limited stock of language, and enabled me to give tongue to many interesting thoughts, which had frequently flashed through my soul, and died away for want of utterance. The mighty power and heart-searching directness of truth, penetrating even the heart of a slaveholder, compelling him to yield up his earthly interests to the claims of eternal justice, were finely illustrated in the dialogue, just referred to; and from the speeches of Sheridan, I got a bold and powerful denunciation of oppression, and a most brilliant vindication of the rights of man. Here was, indeed, a noble acquisition. If I ever wavered under the consideration, that the Almighty, in some way, ordained slavery, and willed my enslavement for his own glory, I wavered no longer. I had now penetrated the secret of all slavery and oppression, and had ascertained their true foundation to be in the pride, the power and the avarice of man. The dialogue and the speeches were all redolent of the principles of liberty, and poured floods of light on the nature and character of slavery. With a book of this kind in my hand, my own human nature, and the facts of my experience, to help me, I was equal to a contest with the religious advocates of slavery, whether among the whites or among the colored people, for blindness, in this matter, is not confined to the former. I have met many religious colored people, at the south, who are under the delusion that God requires them to submit to slavery, and to wear their chains with meekness and humility. I could entertain no such nonsense as this; and I almost lost my patience when I found any colored man weak enough to believe such stuff. Nevertheless, the increase of knowledge was attended with bitter, as well as sweet results. The more I read, the more I was led to abhor and detest slavery, and my enslavers. "Slaveholders," thought I, "are only a band of successful robbers, who left their homes and went into Africa for the purpose of stealing and reducing my people to slavery." I loathed them as the meanest and the most wicked of men. As I read, behold! the very discontent so graphically predicted by Master Hugh, had already come upon me. I was no longer the light-hearted, gleesome boy, full of

mirth and play, as when I landed first at Baltimore. Knowledge had come; light had penetrated the moral dungeon where I dwelt; and,
behold! there lay the bloody whip, for my back,
and here was the iron chain; and my good, *kind
master*, he was the author of my situation. The
revelation haunted me, stung me, and made me
gloomy and miserable. As I writhed under the
sting and torment of this knowledge, I almost
envied my fellow slaves their stupid content-
ment. This knowledge opened my eyes to the
horrible pit, and revealed the teeth of the
frightful dragon that was ready to pounce upon
me, but it opened no way for my escape. I have
often wished myself a beast, or a bird—anything,
rather than a slave. I was wretched and gloomy,
beyond my ability to describe. I was too
thoughtful to be happy. It was this everlasting
thinking which distressed and tormented me;
and yet there was no getting rid of the subject
of my thoughts. All nature was redolent of it.
Once awakened by the silver trump of knowledge, my spirit was roused to eternal wakeful-
ness. Liberty! the inestimable birthright of
every man, had, for me, converted every object
into an asserter of this great right. It was heard
in every sound, and beheld in every object. It
was ever present, to torment me with a sense of
my wretched condition. The more beautiful and
charming were the smiles of nature, the more

horrible and desolate was my condition. I saw nothing without seeing it, and I heard nothing without hearing it. I do not exaggerate, when I say, that it looked from every star, smiled in every calm, breathed in every wind, and moved in every storm.

—1855

The Mill on the Floss

By *GEORGE ELIOT*

AT LAST MAGGIE'S EYES glanced down on the books that lay on the window-shelf, and she half forsook her reverie to turn over listlessly the leaves of the "Portrait Gallery," but she soon pushed this aside to examine the little row of books tied together with string. "Beauties of the Spectator," "Rasselas," "Economy of Human Life," "Gregory's Letter"—she knew the sort of matter that was inside all these: the "Christian year"—that seemed to be a hymn book, and she laid it down again; but *Thomas a Kempis?*—the name had come across her in her reading, and she felt the satisfaction, which every one knows, of getting some ideas to attach to a name that strays solitary in the memory. She took up the little, old, clumsy book with some curiosity; it had the corners turned down in many places, and some hand, now for ever quiet, had made at certain passages strong pen-and-ink marks, long since browned by time. . . .

She read on and on in the old book, devouring eagerly the dialogues with the invisible Teacher, the pattern of sorrow, the source of all strength; returning to it after she had been called away, and reading till the sun went down behind the willows. She knew nothing of doctrines and systems—of mysticism or quietism but this voice out of the far-off middle ages was the direct communication of a human soul's belief and experience, and came to Maggie as an unquestioned message.

I suppose that is the reason why the small old-fashioned book, for which you need only pay sixpence at a book-stall, works miracles to this day, turning bitter waters into sweetness: while expensive sermons and treatises, newly issued, leave all things as they were before. It was written down by a hand that waited for the heart's prompting; it is the chronicle of a solitary, hidden anguish, struggle, trust and triumph —not written on velvet cushions to teach endurance to those who are treading with bleeding feet on the stones. And so it remains to all time a lasting record of human needs and human consolations: the voice of a brother who, ages ago, felt and suffered and renounced—in the cloister, perhaps with serge gown and tonsured head, with much chanting and long fasts, and with a fashion of speech different from ours— but under the same silent far-off heavens, and with the same passionate desires, the same strivings, the same failures, the same weariness.

—1860

His Autobiography

By BENJAMIN FRANKLIN

FROM A CHILD I WAS FOND of reading, and all the little Money that came into my Hands was ever laid out in Books. Pleas'd with the Pilgrim's Progress, my first Collection was of John Bunyan's Works, in separate little Volumes. I afterwards sold them to enable me to buy R. Burton's Historical Collections; they were small Chapmen's Books and cheap, 40 or 50 in all. My Father's little Library consisted chiefly of Books in polemic Divinity, most of which I read, and have since often regretted, that at a time when I had such a Thirst for Knowledge, more proper Books had not fallen in my Way, since it was now resolv'd I should not be a Clergyman. Plutarch's Lives there was, in which I read abundantly, and I still think that time spent to great Advantage. There was also a Book of Defoe's, called an Essay on Projects, and another of Dr. Mather's, call'd Essays to do Good which perhaps gave me a Turn of Thinking that had an Influence on some of the principal future Events of my Life.

This Bookish Inclination at length determin'd my Father to make me a Printer, tho' he had already one Son, (James) of that Profession.

In 1717 my Brother James return'd from England with a Press & Letters to set up his Business in Boston. I lik'd it much better than that
of my Father, but still had a Hankering for the
Sea. To prevent the apprehended Effect of such
an Inclination, my Father was impatient to have
me bound to my Brother. I stood out some time,
but at last was persuaded and signed the Inden-
tures, when I was yet but 12 Years old. I was
to serve as an Apprentice till I was 21 Years of
Age, only I was to be allow'd Journeyman's
Wages during the last Year. In a little time I
made great Proficiency in the Business, and became a useful Hand to my Brother. I now had
Access to better Books. An Acquaintance with
the Apprentices of Booksellers, enabled me
sometimes to borrow a small one, which I was
careful to return soon & clean. Often I sat up in
my Room reading the greatest Part of the Night,
when the Book was borrow'd in the Evening &
to be return'd early in the Morning lest it
should be miss'd or wanted. And after some
time an ingenious Tradesman Mr Matthew
Adams who had a pretty Collection of Books, &
who frequented our Printinghouse, took Notice
of me, invited me to his Library, & very kindly
lent me such Books as I chose to read. I now
took a Fancy to Poetry, and made some little
Pieces. My Brother, thinking it might turn to
account encourag'd me, & put me on composing

two occasional Ballads. One was called the *Light House Tragedy*, & contain'd an Account of the drowning of Capt. Worthilake with his Two Daughters; the other was a Sailor Song on the Taking of *Teach* or Blackbeard the Pirate. They were wretched Stuff, in the Grub-street Ballad Style, and when they were printed he sent me about the Town to sell them. The first sold wonderfully, the Event being recent, having made a great Noise. This flatter'd my Vanity. But my Father discourag'd me, by ridiculing my Performances, and telling me Verse-makers were always Beggars; so I escap'd being a Poet, most probably a very bad one. . . .

My Time for [writing] Exercises & for Reading, was at Night, after Work or before Work began in the Morning; or on Sundays, when I contrived to be in the Printinghouse alone, evading as much as I could the common Attendance on public Worship, which my Father used to exact of me when I was under his Care: And which indeed I still thought a Duty; tho' I could not, as it seemed to me, afford the Time to practise it.

When about 16 Years of Age, I happen'd to meet with a Book, written by one Tryon, recommending a Vegetable Diet. I determined to go into it. My Brother being yet unmarried, did not keep House, but boarded himself & his Ap-

prentices in another Family. My refusing to eat
Flesh occasioned an Inconveniency, and I was
frequently chid for my singularity. I made myself acquainted with Tryon's Manner of prepar-
ing some of his Dishes, such as Boiling Potatoes
or Rice, making Hasty Pudding, & a few others,
and then propos'd to my Brother, that if he
would give me Weekly half the Money he paid
for my Board I would board myself. He instantly agreed to it, and I presently found that I
could save half what he paid me. This was an
additional Fund for buying Books: But I had
another Advantage in it. My Brother and the
rest going from the Printinghouse to their
Meals, I remain'd there alone, and dispatching
presently my light Repast, (which often was no
more than a Biscuit or a Slice of Bread, a Hand-
ful of Raisins or a Tart from the Pastry Cook's,
& a Glass of Water) had the rest of the Time till
their Return, for Study, in which I made the
greater Progress from that greater Clearness of
Head & quicker Apprehension which usually
attend Temperance in Eating & Drinking. And
now it was that being on some Occasion made
asham'd of my Ignorance in Figures, which I
had twice failed in learning when at School, I
took Cocker's Book of Arithmetic, & went thro'
the whole by myself with great Ease. I also read
Seller's & Sturmy's Books of Navigation, &
became acquainted with the little Geometry

they contain, but never proceeded far in that Science. And I read about this Time Locke on Human Understanding, and the Art of Thinking by Messrs du Port Royal.

While I was intent on improving my Language, I met with an English Grammar (I think it was Greenwood's) at the End of which there were two little Sketches of the Arts of Rhetoric and Logic, the latter finishing with a Specimen of a Dispute in the Socratic Method. And soon after I procur'd Xenophon's Memorable Things of Socrates, wherein there are many Instances of the same Method. I was charm'd with it, adopted it, dropped my abrupt Contradiction, and positive Argumentation, and put on the humble Inquirer & Doubter. And being then, from reading Shaftsbury & Collins, become a real Doubter in many Points of our Religious Doctrine, I found this Method safest for myself & very embarrassing to those against whom I used it, therefore I took a Delight in it, practis'd it continually & grew very artful & expert in drawing People even of superior Knowledge into Concessions the Consequences of which they did not foresee, entangling them in Difficulties out of which they could not extricate themselves, and so obtaining Victories that neither myself nor my Cause always deserved....

—1771

Autobiographical Romance

By *MARGARET FULLER*

THERE WAS, IN THE HOUSE, no apartment appropriated to the purpose of a library, but there was in my father's room a large closet filled with books, and to these I had free access when the task-work of the day was done. Its window overlooked wide fields, gentle slopes, a rich and smiling country, whose aspect pleased without much occupying the eye, while a range of blue hills, rising at about twelve miles distance, allured to reverie. . . .

Melancholy attends on the best joys of a merely ideal life, else I should call most happy the hours in the garden, the hours in the book closet. Here were the best French writers of the last century; for my father had been more than half a Jacobin, in the time when the French Republic cast its glare of promise over the world. Here, too, were the Queen Anne authors, his models, and the English novelists; but among them I found none that charmed me. Smollet, Fielding, and the like, deal too broadly with the coarse actualities of life. The best of their men and women—so merely natural, with the nature found every day—do not meet our hopes. Sometimes the simple picture, warm with life and the light of the common son, cannot fail to charm,—as in the wedded love of Fielding's Amelia,—but it is at a later day, when the mind is trained to comparison, that we learn to prize excellence like this as it deserves. Early youth is prince-like: it will bend only to "the king, my father." Various kinds of excellence please, and leave their impression, but the most commanding, alone, is duly acknowledged at that all-exacting age.

Three great authors it was my fortune to meet at this important period,—all, though of unequal, yet congenial powers,—all of rich and wide, rather than aspiring genius,—all free to the extent of the horizon their eye took in,—all fresh with impulse, racy with experience; never to be lost sight of, or superseded, but always to be apprehended more and more.

Ever memorable is the day on which I first took a volume of SHAKSPEARE in my hand to read. It was on a Sunday.

—This day was punctiliously set apart in our house. We had family prayers, for which there was no time on other days. Our dinners were different, and our clothes. We went to church. My father put some limitations on my reading, but—bless him for the gentleness which has left me a pleasant feeling for the day!—he did not pre-scribe what was, but only what was *not*, to be done. And the liberty this left was a large one. "You must not read a novel, or a play;" but all other books, the worst, or the best, were open to me. The distinction was merely technical. The day was pleasing to me, as relieving me from the routine of tasks and recitations; it gave me freer play than usual, and there were fewer things occurred in its course, which reminded me of the divisions of time;

still the church-going, where I heard nothing that had
any connection with my inward life, and these rules,
gave me associations with the day of empty formalities,
and arbitrary restrictions; but though the forbidden book
or walk always seemed more charming then, I was seldom tempted to disobey.—

This Sunday—I was only eight years old—I took
from the bookshelf a volume lettered SHAKSPEARE. It
was not the first time I had looked at it, but before I had
been deterred from attempting to read, by the broken
appearance along the page, and preferred smooth narra-
tive. But this time I held in my hand "Romeo and
Juliet" long enough to get my eye fastened to the page.
It was a cold winter afternoon. I took the book to the
parlor fire, and had there been seated an hour or two,
when my father looked up and asked me what I was
reading so intently. "Shakspeare,"—replied the child,
merely raising her eye from the page. "Shakspeare,—that won't do; that's no book for Sunday; go
put it away and take another." I went as I was bid, but
took no other. Returning to my seat, the unfinished
story, the personages to whom I was but just introduced,
thronged and burnt my brain. I could not bear it long;
such a lure it was impossible to resist. I went and
brought the book again. There were several guests
present, and I had got half through the play before I
again attracted attention. "What is that child about
that she don't hear a word that's said to her?" quoth my
aunt. "What are you reading?" said my father. "Shakspeare" was again the reply, in a clear, though somewhat

impatient, tone. "How?" said my father angrily,—then restraining himself before his guests,—"Give me the book and go directly to bed."

Into my little room no care of his anger followed me. Alone, in the dark, I thought only of the scene placed by the poet before my eye, where the free flow of life, sudden and graceful dialogue, and forms, whether grotesque or fair, seen in the broad lustre of his imagination, gave just what I wanted, and brought home the life I seemed born to live. My fancies swarmed like bees, as I contrived the rest of the story;—what all would do, what say, where go. My confinement tortured me. I could not go forth from this prison to ask after these friends; I could not make my pillow of the dreams about them which yet I could not forbear to frame. Thus was I absorbed when my father entered. He felt it right, before going to rest, to reason with me about my disobedience, shown in a way, as he considered, so insolent. I listened, but could not feel interested in what he said, nor turn my mind from what engaged it. He went away really grieved at my impenitence, and quite at a loss to understand conduct in me so unusual. . . .

My attention thus fixed on Shakspeare, I returned to him at every hour I could command. Here was a counterpoise to my Romans, still more forcible than the little garden. My author could read the Roman nature too,—read it in the sternness of Coriolanus, and in the varied wealth of Caesar. But he viewed these men of will as only one kind of men; he kept them in their place, and I found that he, who could understand the Roman, yet expressed in Hamlet a deeper thought.

In Cervantes, I found far less productive talent,—indeed, a far less powerful genius,—but the same wide wisdom, a discernment piercing the shows and symbols of existence, yet rejoicing in them all, both for their own life, and as signs of the unseen reality. Not that Cervantes philosophized,—his genius was too deeply philosophical for that; he took things as they came before him, and saw their actual relations and bearings. Thus the work he produced was of deep meaning, though he might never have expressed that meaning to himself. It was left implied in the whole. . . .

My third friend was Moliere, one very much lower, both in range and depth, than the others, but, as far as he goes, of the same character. Nothing secluded or partial is there about his genius,—a man of the world, and a man by himself, as he is. It was, indeed, only the poor social world of Paris that he saw, but he viewed it from the firm foundations of his manhood, and every lightest laugh rings from a clear perception, and teaches life anew.

These men were all alike in this,—they loved the *natural history* of man. Not what he should be, but what he is, was the favorite subject of their thought. Whenever a noble leading opened to the eye new paths of light, they rejoiced; but it was never fancy, but always fact, that inspired them. They loved a thorough penetration of the murkiest dens, and most tangled paths of nature; they did not spin from the desires of their own special natures, but reconstructed the world from materials which they collected on every side. Thus their influence upon me was not to prompt me to follow out thought in myself so much as to detect it everywhere, for each of these men is not only a nature, but a happy interpreter of many natures. They taught me to distrust all invention which is not based on a wide experience. Perhaps, too, they taught me to overvalue an outward experience at the expense of inward growth; but all this I did not appreciate till later.

It will be seen that my youth was not unfriended, since those great minds came to me in kindness. A moment of action in one's self, however, is worth an age of apprehension through others; not that our deeds are better, but that they produce a renewal of our being. I have had more productive moments and of deeper joy, but never hours of more tranquil pleasure than those in which these demi-gods visited me,—and with a smile so familiar, that I imagined the world to be full of such. They did me good, for by them a standard was early given of sight and thought, from which I could never go back, and beneath which I cannot suffer patiently my own life or that of any friend to fall. They did me harm, too, for the child fed with meat instead of milk becomes too soon mature. Expectations and desires were thus early raised, after which I must long toil before they can be realized. How poor the scene around, how tame one's own existence, how meagre and faint every power, with these beings in my mind! Often I must cast them quite aside in order to grow in my small way, and not sink into despair. Certainly I do not wish that instead of these masters I had read baby books, written down to children, and with such ignorant dulness that they blunt the senses and corrupt the tastes of the still plastic human being. But I do wish that I had read no books at all till later,—that I had lived with toys, and played in the open air. Children should not cull the fruits of reflection and observation early, but expand in the sun, and let thoughts come to them. They should not through books antedate their actual experiences, but should take them gradually, as sympathy and interpretation are needed. With me, much of life was devoured in the bud. . . .

—1852

The Private Papers
of Henry Ryecroft

By GEORGE GISSING

AS OFTEN AS I SURVEY my bookshelves I am reminded of Lamb's "ragged veterans." Not that all my volumes came from the second-hand stall; many of them were neat enough in new covers; some were even stately in fragrant bindings, when they passed into my hands. But so often have I removed, so rough has been the treatment of my little library at each change of place, and, to tell the truth, so little care have I given to its well-being at normal times (for in all practical matters I am idle and inept), that even the comeliest of my books show the results of unfair usage. More than one has been foully injured by a great nail driven into a packing-case—this but the extreme instance of the wrongs they have undergone. Now that I have leisure and peace of mind, I find myself growing more careful—an illustration of the great truth that virtue is made easy by circumstance. But I confess that, so long as a volume holds together, I am not much troubled as to its outer appearance.

I know men who say they had as lief read any book in a library copy as in one from their own shelf. To me that is unintelligible. For one thing, I know every book of mine by its *scent*, and I have but to put my nose between the pages to be reminded of all sorts of things. My

Gibbon, for example, my well-bound eight-volume Milman edition, which I have read and read and read again for more than thirty years—never do I open it but the scent of the noble page restores to me all the exultant happiness of that moment when I received it as a prize. Or my Shakespeare, the Great Cambridge Shakespeare —it has an odour which carries me yet further back in life; for these volumes belonged to my father, and before I was old enough to read them with understanding, it was often permitted me, as a treat, to take down one of them from the bookcase, and reverently to turn the leaves. The volumes smell exactly as they did in that old time, and what a strange tenderness comes upon me when I hold one of them in hand. For that reason I do not often read Shakespeare in this edition. My eyes being good as ever, I take the Globe volume, which I bought in days when such a purchase was something more than an extravagance; wherefore I regard the book with that peculiar affection which results from sacrifice.

Sacrifice—in no drawing-room sense of the word. Dozens of my books were purchased with money which ought to have been spent upon what are called the necessaries of life. Many a time I have stood before a stall, or a bookseller's window, torn by conflict of intellectual desire and bodily need. At the very hour of dinner, when my stomach clamoured for food, I have been stopped by sight of a volume so long coveted, and marked at so advantageous a price, that I *could* not let it go; yet to buy it meant pangs of famine. My Heyne's *Tibullus* was grasped at such a moment. It lay on the stall of the old

book-shop in Goodge Street—a stall where now and then
one found an excellent thing among quantities of rubbish.
Sixpence was the price—sixpence! At that time I used to
eat my midday meal (of course my dinner) at a coffee-
shop in Oxford Street, one of the real old coffee-shops,
such as now, I suppose, can hardly be found. Sixpence
was all I had—yes, all I had in the world; it would purchase a plate of meat and vegetables. But I did not dare
to hope that the *Tibullus* would wait until the morrow,
when a certain small sum fell due to me. I paced the
pavement, fingering the coppers in my pocket, eyeing the
stall, two appetites at combat within me. The book was
bought and I went home with it, and as I made a dinner
of bread and butter I gloated over the pages.

In this *Tibullus* I found pencilled on the last page:
"Perlegi, Oct. 4, 1792." Who was that possessor of the
book, nearly a hundred years ago? There was no other
inscription. I like to imagine some poor scholar, poor
and eager as I myself, who bought the volume with drops
of his blood, and enjoyed the reading of it even as I did.
How much *that* was I could not easily say. Gentle-
hearted Tibullus!—of whom there remains to us a poet's
portrait more delightful, I think, than anything of the
kind in Roman literature.

> *An tacitum silvas inter reptare*
> *salubres,*
> *Curantem quidquid dignum sapiente*
> *bonoque est?*

So with many another book on the thronged shelves.

To take them down is to recall, how vividly, a struggle
and a triumph. In those days money represented nothing
to me, nothing I cared to think about, but the acquisition
of books. There were books of which I had passionate
need, books more necessary to me than bodily nourish-
ment. I could see them, of course, at the British Museum,
but that was not at all the same thing as having and
holding them, my own property, on my own shelf. Now
and then I have bought a volume of the raggedest and
wretchedest aspect, dishonoured with foolish scribbling,
torn, blotted—no matter, I liked better to read out of
that than out of a copy that was not mine. But I was
guilty at times of mere self-indulgence; a book tempted
me, a book which was not one of those for which I really
craved, a luxury which prudence might bid me forgo. As,
for instance, my *Jung-Stilling*. It caught my eye in
Holywell Street; the name was familiar to me in *Wahr-
heit und Dichtung*, and curiosity grew as I glanced
over the pages. But that day I resisted. In truth, I
could not afford the eighteen-pence, which means that
just then I was poor indeed. Twice again did I pass, each
time assuring myself that *Jung-Stilling* had found no
purchaser. There came a day when I was in funds. I see
myself hastening to Holywell Street (in those days my
habitual pace was five miles an hour), I see the little grey
old man with whom I transacted my business—what was
his name?—the bookseller who had been, I believe, a
Catholic priest, and still had a certain priestly dignity
about him. He took the volume, opened it, mused for a
moment, then, with a glance at me, said, as if thinking

aloud: "Yes, I wish I had time to read it."

Sometimes I added the labour of a porter to my fasting endured for the sake of books. At the little shop near Portland Road Station I came upon a first edition of Gibbon, the price an absurdity—I think it was a shilling a volume. To possess those clean-paged quartos I would have sold my coat. As it happened, I had not money enough with me, but sufficient at home. I was living at Islington. Having spoken with the bookseller, I walked home, took the cash, walked back back again, and—carried the tomes from the west end of Euston Road to a street in Islington far beyond the *Angel*. I did it in two journeys—this being the only time in my life when I thought of Gibbon in avoirdupois. Twice—three times reckoning the walk for the money—did I descend Euston Road and climb Pentonville on that occasion. Of the season and the weather I have no recollection; my joy in the purchase I had made drove out every other thought. Except, indeed, of the weight. I had infinite energy, but not much muscular strength, and the end of the last journey saw me upon a chair, perspiring, flaccid, aching—exultant!

The well-to-do person would hear this story with astonishment. Why did I not get the bookseller to send me the volumes? Or, if I could not wait, was there no omnibus along that London highway? How could I make the well-to-do person understand that I did not feel able to afford, that day, one penny more than I had spent on the book? No, no, such labour-saving expenditure did not come within my scope; whatever I enjoyed I earned it,

literally, by the sweat of my brow. In those days I hardly
knew what it was to travel by omnibus. I have walked
London streets for twelve and fifteen hours together
without ever a thought of saving my legs, or my time, by
paying for waftage. Being poor as poor can be, there
were certain things I had to renounce, and this was one of
them.

Years after, I sold my first edition of Gibbon for even
less than it cost me; it went with a great many other fine
books in folio and quarto, which I could not drag about
with me in my constant removals; the man who bought
them spoke of them as "tomb-stones." Why has Gibbon
no market value? Often has my heart ached with regret
for those quartos. The joy of reading the *Decline and
Fall* in that fine type! The page was appropriate to the
dignity of the subject; the mere sight of it tuned one's
mind. I suppose I could easily get another copy now; but
it would not be to me what that other was, with its
memory of dust and toil.

There must be several men of spirit and experiences
akin to mine who remember that little bookshop opposite
Portland Road Station. It had a peculiar character; the
books were of a solid kind—chiefly theology and classics
—and for the most part those old editions which are
called worthless, which have no bibliopolic value, and
have been supplanted for practical use by modern issues.
The bookseller was very much a gentleman, and this
singular fact, together with the extremely low prices at
which his volumes were marked, sometimes inclined me

to think that he kept the shop for mere love of letters. Things in my eyes inestimable I have purchased there for a few pence, and I don't think I ever gave more than a shilling for any volume. As I once had the opportunity of perceiving, a young man fresh from class-rooms could only look with wondering contempt on the antiquated stuff which it rejoiced me to gather from that kindly stall, or from the richer shelves within. My *Cicero's Letters* for instance: podgy volumes in parchment, with all the notes of Graevius, Gronovius, and I know not how many other old scholars. Pooh! Hopelessly out of date. But I could never feel that. I have a deep affection for Graevius and Gronovius and the rest, and if I knew as much as they did, I should be well satisfied to rest under the young man's disdain. The zeal of learning is never out of date; the example—were there no more—burns before one as a sacred fire, for ever unquenchable. In what modern editor shall I find such love and enthusiasm as glows in the annotations of old scholars?

Even the best editions of our day have so much of the mere schoolbook; you feel so often that the man does not regard his author as literature, but simply as text. Pedant for pedant, the old is better than the new. . . .

—1903

An Essay in Apology

By *EDMUND GOSSE*

MY LITTLE "CLOSET" OF BOOKS is none of those magnificent collections which thrill America from New York to Texas and on to California. It does not compete with the British Museum nor with the Ashley Library. But I dare to claim for it that it is extremely *personal*. It represents the tastes, the habits, the limitations, and the requirements of the owner. It is the accretion of more than half a century of effort originally directed not towards the creation of a library but towards the furniture of a mind. I have collected books not, in the main, because they were rare or curious, but because I wanted to read them at my leisure, and to have them at my side for reference. Other considerations have intervened. There has grown up a certain pride in seeing that these companions and helpers were in wholesome condition, and clothed in appropriate garments. I have come to take a pride in their "state" and a care for their pedigree. In short, the voracious reader has almost unconsciously developed into a collector, yet without ever ceasing to be essentially a reader. I have never added books to my shelves for purposes of mere ornament of binding or peculiarity of imprint, although I admit these objects to be legitimate. They do not happen to appeal to me. On the other hand, my books have never been so numerous as to make it difficult to refer to them all upon occasion, and there is, I think, not one with which I am not on easy terms.

If I may be forgiven for the fatuity of speaking of my own childhood, I will begin at the beginning by telling my indulgent reader that my bibliophily was discerned in the age of bib and tucker, since it has been handed down that, refraining until rather late from such elements of speech as "Mama" and "gee-gee," the earliest word I was known to utter was "book," laying my hand upon a specimen to show what I meant. I had the odd fortune, at my start in life, to be appointed a transcriber or copying clerk in the Department of Printed Books in the British Museum. Fifty-seven years ago, this was not the admirably equipped and neatly disciplined institution which students know and value to-day. Great laxity prevailed among the assistants and librarians, whose standard of accuracy was low, and their zeal that of the Church of Laodicea. If attempts were made to stir these drones, the reply was obvious that they were so meanly paid and so villainously housed that neither activity nor assiduity could be expected from them. Into this dull hive I was thrust, a young bee as idle as the best of them; I have nothing to say here of the queer, even grotesque conditions of life in that mysterious fortress or cage of steel and leather in which my days were spent. But one advantage, unforeseen by those who appointed and those who neglected me, pursued my official indolence.

When the very small amount of work demanded from the slaves, by slave-drivers even lazier than them-

selves, had been performed, we transcribers in the Printed
Book Department enjoyed an almost unlimited leisure.
Cricket was not unpractised in remoter galleries; less
audacious spirits cultivated the pencil or the jew's-harp.
My own diversion was reading, ceaseless devouring of
the printed page. I believe that the Library is nowadays
—I am sure very properly—closed to youths of seventeen
or eighteen, but there was no one then to check me or say
me nay. Through the long silent afternoons, immersed in
the curious odour of slowly decaying calf-skin, I would
stand in the upper gallery of the King's Library or among
the Garrick Plays, absorbing with ceaseless appetite the
obscurer parts of seventeenth-century literature. Treasures of the most unique description were open to the air in
those easy days. Such recognised rarities as were already
put under glass and locked up were scarcely less open to
access, since, although we were strictly forbidden to touch
the keys, I knew where they were kept and used them
without scruple. What a world of wonder was unveiled to
me in those long hours, when, if a bookworm had been
there, I could have started at his cock-crow, and where
not a footfall broke the velvet silence! There I read the
poets and playwrights who were as yet entirely inedited;
there, in the dim quartos—many of them a good deal cut
down as I regretfully remember—I made such friends as
Peele and Vaughan and Cartwright, and such life-long
acquaintances as Cyril Tourneur.

During these early years I lacked not merely the
money but even the inclination to collect a library. With
the ancient world open to me in the Department of

Printed Books, and with a subscription to the modern world at Mr. Mudie's, I might have gone through life without a volume in my possession. But when, in 1875, I ceased to belong to the British Museum, and opened for the first time a modest home of my own, all this was changed, and a new appetite was created. I forget what French bibliophil it is who says, "Studying at public libraries is like staying at an inn." This is true, and books are not entirely valued or intimately loved unless they are ranged about us as we sit at home.

With my extremely small resources, the buying of expensive volumes was out of the question, but there was a field open to me fifty years ago which is closed to the poor student to-day. I was particularly led to make an examination of what are called Restoration Plays— that is to say, of the English dramatic literature pro- duced between 1660 and 1700. That span of forty years was remarkably rich in a drama that in Victorian times had scarcely been explored, and that lay under the ban of those who exalted the Elizabethan and Jacobean ages inordinately. The Restoration was supposed to be uniformly lacking in decency and merit. The dramatists were for the most part inedited, and to refer to their text it was needful to procure original or contemporary edi- tions, which were almost without exception in the form of quarto pamphlets. The earliest play I bought, and the beginning of my collection, was a clean tall copy of Southerne's "The Loyal Brother," of 1682. The prologue and epilogue, though there is nothing to show it, were written by Dryden for this, Southerne's earliest publication. I remember that I had to pay the bookseller half a crown, which I thought extortionate.

Some time elapsed before I began to make a persistent search for plays in the shops of the second-hand booksellers. I think I was really started on my enterprise by going casually into a shop in Soho, where I remarked, with the hunter's excitement, that the counter was heaped with quarto plays of the seventeenth century. I felt like the African traveller who suddenly comes upon a water-hole surrounded by all the beasts of the wilderness drinking together in unity. The explanation of the phenomenon was that the bookseller—I forgot his name—had just bought *en bloc* the library of a Mr. John Kershaw, who had, apparently, indulged a particular fancy for plays. These had been suddenly delivered to the purchaser, who must have bought them like a pig in a poke, for he seemed to know nothing of their relative value, and was only anxious to get rid of them for a percentage of profit. There were treasures lying in that ignominious heap, and if I had only had in my pocket what a single one of some of those plays would fetch to-day, I might have gone off laden with spoil. There were things lying there which, in all the fifty years since, I have never cast eyes upon again. I emptied my poor purse, however, to its uttermost penny, and I carried away a goodly parcel, containing, amongst other jewels, the earliest 1664 issue of Sir George Etheredge's "The Comical Revenge; or Love in a Tub," of which (I believe) no other copy had at that time been met with.

The importance of this play in the history of English drama gave interest to the discovery of its date, which had hitherto been placed in 1668.

With gratitude I recall the kindness of the various booksellers whose premises I haunted ; most of them endured with indulgent patience the rummaging of their top-shelves by an unprofitable lad. I recall in particular Mr. Wilson of Great Russell Street, where my very earliest investigations were made. His was a stern, grim figure, calculated to alarm more than to seduce the would-be purchaser, yet he was very affable to me. I remember that Mr. Wilson gave me a piece of advice, at which the book-buyers of the present day will smile. Entering into my passion for plays, he said, "Those Restoration dramas of yours will never have the slightest value, but you keep your eye on Massinger and Ford. You may think it extravagant, but I recommend you not to grudge ten shilling apiece for a really fine copy of a first edition of them, or of Shirley or any other of those chaps. They may not be worth it now, but they will be one of these days." . . .

The name of Salkeld has escaped my pen. It should have come a little later, for I did not find that remarkable bower of dust and beauty, his shop in Red Lion Square, until about 1876. I was taken there by my earliest master in the science of bibliography, the poet John Leicester Warren, long afterwards the third Lord Tabley. He was a book-man without guile, and it was first from him that I learned what book-collecting involved. Warren would think nothing of hanging

about Red Lion Square at six in the morning, waiting
for Salkeld to take down his shutters. In Warren I
first observed the passion of the genuine bibliophil, and
I imbibed from him the true spirit of the game. I have
seen him physically faint with joy at securing an
"Alastor" of 1816, and tears spring to his eyes at the
unexpected arrival of a Milton's "Poems" of 1645. In one
of his own poems he celebrates the charms of Red Lion
Square and of

> Salkeld, solace once of book-men,
>   Now beyond all cabs and ken,
> Far removed in realms transpontine,
>   Who shall find his haunts again?

Who, indeed! and where are the roses of yesteryear?

The premises of Mr. Salkeld were extensive, upstairs
and downstairs, and they were lumbered beyond the
dreams of the most untidy of bookworms. With great
difficulty the visitor penetrated between tables heaped
with miscellaneous literature and shelves which bulged
with volumes two or three deep. An inner parlour was
the haunt of the bibliopole himself, who had cleared one
chair and the corner of one table for his practical requirements. Elsewhere chaos reigned, but Mr. Salkeld's
memory was wonderful. He would point to a
tottering tower of books and say, "Somewhere at
the back of that there's a Giles Fletcher if you
want to see it. Got no half-title, though!" Upstairs even the memory of Mr. Salkeld was at fault.
Here there was no order, no tables, only piles of books on

broken kitchen chairs; and hanging from the ceiling a large open cage of doves. Mr. Salkeld soon gave me his confidence, and I was allowed to rout at my own free will in the upper rooms. But the doves were a trial. Bored with their long seclusion, they used to leave their cage to greet the visitor. In those days the humblest of us wore a silk hat on all occasions. Just as one was stooping to detach a folio from its heap, a dove would make a sudden swoop, and skate wildly on one's hat, which would presently skip off into a corner carrying the hysterical bird upon its rim. Despite the doves and the dirt, many a precious item have I excavated in the garrets at Red Lion Square. There are no such treasure-heaps left unsearched to-day in the sophisticated shops of Soho. . . .

Leicester Warren was accustomed to urge upon me the importance of having a book-plate of my own. I was not eager for it, but in 1883 our ingenious friend, Edwin Abbey, undertook to make designs for Austin Dobson's books and for mine. Each of his drawings was charming; mine represented a cavalier of the period of Charles I., in lovely garments, walking in the open air and holding a manuscript in front of him. The sun, an enormous luminary, is blazing at his back, and the motto is "Gravis cantantibus umbra"; why I chose this, and where I found it, are details which have escaped me, but I imagine it meant that poets carry no sunshades.

This spirited and picturesque design was very successfully engraved, and I began to paste it in the more precious of my books. This labour, however, I found distasteful, and the dampness produced a tendency to cockling of the fly-leaves. What, however, really made me desist was the senseless rage of collectors of *ex-libris*. That I possessed a book-plate designed by so celebrated an artist as Edwin Abbey induced complete strangers to ask me to give them specimens of it. Many would actually enclose their own "in exchange." This filled me with what I still consider a just anger. I had no sort of use for the book-plates of these volunteers, which found their way to the wastepaper basket; and as to giving my own to a stranger, that would have been to stultify the whole proceeding. One's book-plate is, or should remain, a jealously guarded personal possession. Once separate the book-plate from the book of its owner and its whole significance is gone. The only reason for using a book-plate is to issue a final claim to property in the book. I am afraid that some collectors of *ex-libris*, especially in America, thought me coarse when I replied that I would no more send away my book-plates than I would my flannel waistcoats; both were individual possessions with which no stranger should meddle. What finally prejudiced me, however, against the hoarders of other people's book-plates was the discovery that there are fiends in human shape who take a book and remove its plate with steam, in order to place it in their ridiculous "collection." My amusing friend, Lady Dorothy Nevill, preserved her library by pasting in each volume the plain legend: "This book has been stolen from Lady Dorothy Nevill." This was drastic, but practical.

My feeling about bindings is very different. The

theory that a jewel deserves a jewel-case is one which I
share, I suppose, with every genuine lover of books.
No one would enjoy more than I should to contemplate on my shelves a Montaigne printed by Abel
Langelier and bound with the arms of the Count
d'Hoym, but really to revel in this kind of bibliophily
it is needful to be wealthy and a Frenchman. Bindings
have been a consolation to many a public man who
found that the world was out of joint. It is said that
whenever Jules Janin had made a more than usually
egregious blunder in his weekly article, and had been
ridiculed in consequence—when, for instance, he
had described the lobster as the Cardinal of the
Seas, or Smyrna as one of the Greek islands—he would
rush upstairs and fondle his first editions bound in
crushed levant by Cape or Bauzonnet. They never
failed to soothe him. But an affecting and chronic
want of pounds has always precluded me me from
purchasing such white elephants. I have been obliged
to confine myself to encasing particular favourites in
the sobriety of plain morocco, by Bedford sometimes,
by Riviere or De Coverly as a rule; while, since the
war, the enormous rise in prices has deprived me of
even this chaste indulgence. I comfort myself by
thinking that in most cases nothing is so completely
satisfactory as the well-preserved original covers in
which the volume first saw the light. What can be
more delightful than Keats or Landor in the impli-
cit simplicity of plain covers with paper labels? To
preserve these intact, Mr. Bain has made me cloth

boxes, sometimes lined with thin flannel, and lettered outside to look like volumes. Thus ensconced, the book defies not merely dust and exposure, but the wear and tear of circulation.

The importance of my collection is not to be insisted upon. Mine is essentially the workshop and playground of a man of letters. These books have been my tools and are still my companions. He who turns Mr. Cox's pages will be able to judge for himself how I collected them and why. There are no Shakespeare quartos here nor vellum Hours printed at the Unicorn. Curiosities, I hope, a few, but no real rarities in the heroic sense, will be discovered among the ensuing entries. Nor could La Bruyere—as he so rudely does of some collectors in his essay *De la Mode*—complain of me that my room stinks like a tannery with the richness of my stamped leathers. There are good books here, and uncommon books, but it may be that you must love them, as I have done, e'er to you they seem books worthy to be loved.

The exiguity of my purse was long my misery, but I have come to look upon it as my consolation also. Boethius, surely, did not live in vain. There is a pleasure incident to the collector even in his poverty. Many years ago there was to be sold a little eighteenth-century treasure which I had long desired, and it seemed going at a quiet auction. But, alas! the Exxl of Rxxxxxxy had heard of it, and I fell before him, like a reed, at my first bid. I try to support the blows of life with fortitude, but I confess that on this occasion I dropped a tear on the shoulder of the most judicious of bibliopoles, now long departed. "He gets everything," I moaned; "he was born to get everything." "No," replied Mr. B., "not everything. He has not, and never will have, the exquisite pleasure of buying what he knows he cannot afford."

Of my seventeenth-century and eighteenth-century possessions enough is said in the ensuing pages. But a section of my library of even more special interest is the record of what is nowadays called "association." In selecting books of the present and immediate past, Mr. Cox has been guided not so much by the rarity of the issue as by the fact of its enshrining some personal and individual memory. In the latter case danger from fire, which hangs forever like a menace over the imagination of the collector, is greatly intensified. If a first edition of Walton or Pascal is destroyed, the loss is very serious, but it is not irreparable. Money might restore what is gone. But if a great dead poet has written your name and his in a volume, if he has made a relic for you by some expression of feeling or by some improvised jest, and if that is destroyed, no Bonanza King, with millions in his bank, can restore the treasure.

My recent books are largely records of friendships which are the most sacred memories of my life, and which the passage of years can but continue to sanctify with accessions of vain regret. When ambition sinks to a close, and we are left with so many presumptuous hopes un-realised, so little done of all we gaily started out to do, I am not sure that much will be more consoling than to have at hand the proof that those who passed us in the race regarded us, while the race was being run, with esteem, and sometimes with affection. If I have taken the egotistic step of allowing this catalogue to be published, it is most of all that it may preserve, against the possibility of extinction, these precious memorials of friendship. At least my children shall discover that I have possessed the confidence of men and women whose praise is better than rubies—yes, and better than all the manuscripts in the Vatican.

—1923

On Giving Books

By STEPHANIE GREENE

WHEN I GIVE A GIFT, it is usually a book. They are a pleasure to wrap, won't leak in your suitcase and are difficult to break. For wedding gifts, I generally give cookbooks or dictionaries so the happy couple will be able to feed themselves with imagination and settle Scrabble disputes before they get divisive. My current favorites are *The New Basics Cookbook*, by Julee Rosso and Sheila Lukins, because everything in it turns out well, and *The American Heritage Dictionary* because I like the pictures in the margins. My newest discovery is *New Traditions*, by Susan Abel Lieberman, which is about imaginative ways to celebrate holidays and milestones—perfect for couples happily reinventing those wheels.

I like to give books to children because a well-storied childhood can provide the basis for a broad education of both mind and heart. A book is also the most likely present to survive a children's birthday party undestroyed. Once my husband and I were invited to the fourth birthday party of a charming little boy we met on the train going to Santa Fe. Not seeing a toy store downtown, we went to a wonderful bookstore there, *Altiplano* (High Plains). We bought a copy of Peter Spier's *People* because the boy was very social and curious about the world. Arriving at the party, we were ushered into the kitchen where the stainless steel sink held gallons of dubious looking cherry Koolaid. The boy's father, apparently unprepared for the energy level at this party, stood by in shock as his son tore through presents and Playdough was ground into the beige carpet. But *People* was intact when we left, so perhaps Adam, the boy, later had an opportunity to enjoy it.

As a child, I was given many delightful books: *Babar*, *Madeline*, *Stuart Little*, *The Little Princess*, and *D'Aulaire's Greek Myths*. From them I learned that books could expand my world with points of view vastly different from my own, rather like having colorful, hospitable and infinitely tolerant friends who could be summoned at will. It was a startling and exciting discovery.

My father, a publisher and bookstore owner for twenty-five years, was an inspired book giver. It was he who taught me the joy of giving books. He was always buying books. Whenever we went into someone else's bookstore, he would announce that we "should buy something to encourage these nice people." This happened in stores ranging in size from the smallest, where his sale would be the only one in the course of a day, to the grandest, such as Rizzolis in New York. I would dutifully load up and we would present the stack to the cashier. He never edited my pile in any way. What a wonderful sense of possibility! What generosity! He regarded books as a totally delicious necessity, much as if birthday cake were to be found to be the most perfectly nutritious food.

From the pleasure of ownership followed the pleasure of giving books to others. I bought books for my father because he was so easily pleased. A biography of Noel Coward, *The John Collier Reader*, almost anything on Venice or Venetians, books on topiary or photography, okapis or Sir Walter Scott—his taste was eclectic and passionate. He constantly bought books not only for others but for himself, but in doing so, never became any more difficult to please. It was so much fun getting him books that I never really lost the habit. Even a decade after his death, I still come upon a book that I know he'd have enjoyed.

Most active bibliophiles present a more formidable front to the gift-giver. I was browsing in a newly opened bookstore and asked the owner to show me books on interior design. He asked me whom the book was for, and did I have anything specific in mind. I replied it was for my husband who, as the harried father of two delightful children, needed, at the end of a day, to feast his eyes on a tranquil and elegant domestic scene. I would explore the section and find a surprise for him. The owner then confided that the thing he most regretted about having a bookstore was that no one bought *him* books anymore. No doubt intimidated, his friends assumed he had everything he wanted, and if he didn't possess a book, he must have already seen and dismissed it. He said he missed the excitement of having someone put a wonderful new find in his hands. He sounded quite forlorn at the prospect of having to discover every new book on his own.

I don't blame him. At its best, giving books is giving someone a world. To be giving Maxine Hong Kingston's *Woman Warrior* is to discover an intelligent point of view so different from my own, and so compelling, that my world is enlarged forever by reading it. For the same reason, if I could get hold of the biography of Lobsang Rampa, *The Third Eye*, about the Tibetan monk's astonishing apprenticeship (I believe it's out of print) I would give it away indiscriminately.

Everyone has presents to give. But if I have an advantage in this area, where books are concerned, it's that I have worked with books for a fair part of my life; in a publishing house, in bookstores, and as a librarian —more or less as a paid browser, to tell the truth. Over the years, friends and family have even flattered me into believing that I give them interesting books. My mother paid me a compliment I will cherish above all her others when she told me I gave her the best books. This was upon receiving *Beloved*, Toni Morrison's masterpiece, a gift-giving coup that will not easily be duplicated.

I have also made horrendous mistakes, and my most spectacular also involved my mother: I gave her a book to while away her first plane trip since my father's death in a plane crash. It was a whodunnit, her favorite genre. Unfortunately it was the Elmore Leonard which begins with a twenty-page description of an embalming. Among my mother's fine points is a forgiving nature, at least toward her children.

I am stumped by my husband, a brilliant reader and

opinionated trawler through discount book catalogues, notably The Scholar's Bookshelf, as well as a regular peruser of bookstores in three cities. He can find and digest tomes on the archeology of beekeeping, street cries in old London, and lobstering slang within the space of a week. I have yet to really surprise and delight him, opening the door on an entirely new enthusiasm, but am determined to keep trying.

What makes for a bullseye? Discovery. If someone can be introduced to a new author, book, topic or slant on a topic, I am at my happiest, a matchmaker invited to the wedding. The spark is in imaginative introduction: with books it is possible to match a person more closely than with any other gift. I prefer that inspiration to slogging through jumbled used book bins for an elusive final addition to a set: like sending away for odd pieces of china, perhaps surer to please, yet somehow less exciting.

My Russian friend, Lena, living and studying in Moscow, posed a delightful challenge: a student of English and French, well-read, generous and kind, requested recent American literature. So I asked myself which modern American writers would represent the best of fiction in the last ten years? After compiling a list that would have cost me several hundred dollars to send, even by slow boat, I settled on *Cathedral* by Raymond Carver, *Ironweed*, by William Kennedy, and *Beloved*, even though the dialects in the latter may prove too difficult. Next will possibly be *Ceremony*, by Leslie Marmon Silko and *Love Medicine* by Louise

Erdrich.

But there are certain favorite books that I have yet to give. *The Periodic Table*, by Primo Levi, is an elegant book of friendship. In it, Levi's friends are likened to elements in the Periodic Table. It is not the easiest match to bring off. The recipient would best be a scientist, fascinated by the mysteries of friendship, and not disheartened by knowledge of Levi's own suicide. The delightful *Swallowing Clouds*, by A. Zee, which teaches Chinese characters using restaurant menus, is another match. Most of my friends like Chinese food and language, but wouldn't it call for a particular zeal for them to remember the character for fire in all its permutations through every demanding, though enchanting, chapter? Or if I gave *Care of the Soul*, by Thomas Moore, which provides a wise, soothing yet highly provocative read—almost like a good retreat in itself—would my friends feel too prosletized?

To be honest, the main reason I give books is sheer bossiness. When I was less careful, in my youth, I would stumble upon a book I loved and then give it to everyone on my list. 1980 was the year of *Living Your Dreams*, by Gayle Delaney—actually a very good manual on understanding and using one's sleeping dreams. Wouldn't everyone's life be improved, I thought, if they could do this? I can, and mine was, or so the reasoning went. I waited for the ecstatic thanks to pour in, but in vain. My friends, troopers to the last, thought it, in varying degrees, interesting; a few tried it out, but they did not all emerge radiant from their sleep, problems solved,

worlds conquered. Lesson: people have their own histories, chemistries and causes. When this realization finally
hit me, rather late, it was then astounding to me that any
two people could enjoy the same book.

With this realization, I have tempered my inscrip-
tions. Not all presents are bullseyes, and sometimes my
presents are given away. How embarrassing to have to
deal with lavish sentiments written in permanent ink.
What can be done? Rip out the page, thereby loosening
another page in the signature, or wield a heavy magic
marker, or just resign oneself to losing a bit of privacy (I
have heard that very fine sandpaper does a serviceable
job of removing ink, but have yet to resort to it)? It is
better to leave the book until summoned by the delighted
receiver to inscribe. Even so the book may get the heave-
ho in a few years, regardless. We are a restless people. I
should have inured myself to the mutability of life, and
of book collections, long before this. But I haven't.

I expect people not only to keep, but to treasure the
books I give them. Forever. If I find too many of my
presents at the local bargain bin, or given to mutual
acquaintances, I take undue umbrage. When it becomes
clear that someone doesn't appreciate my book presents,
he starts getting flavored vinegars for Christmas. Na-
sturtium is the prettiest, as long as one remembers to
strain out those few dawdling earwigs.

—1993

On Reading Old Books

By WILLIAM HAZLITT

I HATE TO READ NEW BOOKS. There are twenty or thirty volumes that I have read over and over again, and these are the only ones that I have any desire ever to read at all. It was a long time before I could bring myself to sit down to the *Tales of My Landlord*, but now that author's works have made a considerable addition to my scanty library. I am told that some of Lady Morgan's are good, and have been recommended to look into *Anastasius*; but I have not yet ventured upon that task. A lady, the other day, could not refrain from expressing her surprise to a friend, who said he had been reading *Delphine*:—she asked,—If it had not been published some time back? Women judge of books as they do of fashions or complexions, which are admired only "in their newest gloss." That is not my way. I am not one of those who trouble the circulating libraries much, or pester the booksellers for mail-coach copies of standard periodical publications. I cannot say that I am greatly addicted to black-letter, but I profess myself well versed in the marble bindings of Andrew Millar, in the middle of the last century; nor does my taste revolt at Thurlow's *State Papers*, in russia leather; or an ample impression of Sir William Temple's *Essays*, with a portrait after Sir Godfrey Kneller in front. I do not think altogether the worse of a book for having survived the author a generation or two. I have more confidence in the dead than the living. Contemporary writers may generally be divided into two classes—one's friends or one's foes. Of the first we are compelled to think too well, and of the last we are disposed to think too ill, to receive much genuine pleasure from the perusal, or to judge fairly of the merits of either. One candidate for literary fame, who happens to be of our acquaintance, writes finely, and like a man of genius; but unfortunately has a foolish face, which spoils a delicate passage; another inspires us with the highest respect for his personal talents and character, but does not quite come up to our expectations in print. All these contradictions and petty details interrupt the calm current of our reflections. If you want to know what any of the authors were who lived before our time, and are still objects of anxious inquiry, you have only to look into their works. But the dust and smoke and noise of modern literature have nothing in common with the pure, silent air of immortality.

When I take up a work that I have read before (the oftener the better), I know what I have to expect. The satisfaction is not lessened by being anticipated. When the entertainment is altogether new, I sit down to it as I should to a strange dish—turn and pick out a bit here and there, and am in doubt what to think of the composition. There is a want of confidence and security to second appetite. New-fangled books are also like made-dishes in this respect, that they are generally little else

than hashes and *rifaceimenti* of what has been served
up entire and in a more natural state at other times.
Besides, in thus turning to a well-known author, there is
not only an assurance that my time will not be thrown
away, or my palate nauseated with the most insipid or
vilest trash, but I shake hands with, and look an old,
tried, and valued friend in the face, compare notes, and
chat the hours away. It is true, we form dear friendships
with such ideal guests—dearer, alas! and more lasting,
than those with our most intimate acquaintance. In
reading a book which is an old favourite with me (say
the first novel I ever read) I not only have the pleasure
of imagination and of a critical relish of the work,
but the pleasures of memory added to it. It recalls the
same feelings and associations which I had in first reading it, and which I can never have again in any other
way. Standard productions of this kind are links in the
chain of our conscious being. They bind together the
different scattered divisions of our personal identity
They are landmarks and guides in our journey throug.
life. They are pegs and loops on which we can hang up,
or from which we can take down, at pleasure, the ward-
robe of a moral imagination, the relics of our best affec-
tions, the tokens and records of our happiest hours. They
are "for thoughts and for remembrance!" They are like
Fortunatus's Wishing Cap—they give us the best riches
—those of Fancy; and transport us, not over half the
globe, but (which is better) over half our lives, at a
word's notice!

My father Shandy solaced himself with Bruscambille. Give me for this purpose a volume of *Peregrine Pickle* or *Tom Jones*. Open either of them anywhere—at the Memoirs of Lady Vane, or the adventures at the masquerade with Lady Bellaston, or the disputes between Thwackum and Square, or the escape of Molly Seagrim, or the incident of Sophia and her muff, or the edifying prolixity of her aunt's lecture—and there I find the same delightful, busy, bustling scene as ever, and feel myself the same as when I was first introduced into the midst of it. Nay, sometimes the sight of an odd volume of these good old English authors on a stall, or the name lettered on the back among others on the shelves of a library, answers the purpose, revives the whole train of ideas, and sets "the puppets dallying." Twenty years are struck off the list, and I am a child again. A sage philosopher, who was not a very wise man, said, that he should like very well to be young again, if he could take his experience along with him. This ingenious person did not seem to be aware, by the gravity of his remark, that the great advantage of being young is to be without this weight of experience, which he would fain place upon the shoulders of youth, and which never comes too late with years. Oh! what a privilege to be able to let this hump, like Christian's burthen, drop from off one's back, and transport oneself, by the help of a little musty duodecimo, to the time when "ignorance was bliss," and when we first got a peep at the raree-show of the world, through the glass of fiction—gazing at mankind, as we do at wild beasts in a menagerie, through the bars of their cages—or at cur-

iosities in a museum, that we must not touch! For myself, not only are the old ideas of the contents of the work
brought back to my mind in all their vividness, but the
old associations of the faces and persons of those I then
knew, as they were in their lifetime—the place where I
sat to read the volume, the day when I got it, the feeling
of the air, the fields, the sky return, and all my early
impressions with them. This is better to me—those
places, those times, those persons, and those feelings that
come across me as I retrace the story and devour the
page, are to me better far than the wet sheets of the last
new novel from the Ballantyne press, to say nothing of
the Minerva press in Leadenhall Street. It is like visiting
the scenes of early youth. I think of the time "when I
was in my father's house, and my path ran down with
butter and honey"—when I was a little, thoughtless
child, and had no other wish or care but to con my daily
task, and be happy! *Tom Jones*, I remember, was the
first work that broke the spell. It came down in numbers
once a fortnight, in Cooke's pocket-edition, embellished
with cuts. I had hitherto read only in school-books, and
a tiresome ecclesiastical history (with the exception of
Mrs. Radcliffe's *Romance of the Forest*): but this had
a different relish with it—"sweet in the mouth," though
not "bitter in the belly." It smacked of the world I lived
in, and in which I was to live—and showed me groups,
"gay creatures" not "of the element," but of the earth;
not "living in the clouds," but travelling the same
road that I did;—some that had passed on before me,
and others that might soon overtake me. My heart had

palpitated at the thoughts of a boarding-school ball, or gala-day at Midsummer or Christmas: but the world I had found out in Cooke's edition of the *British Novelists* was to me a dance through life, a perpetual gala-day. The sixpenny numbers of this work regularly contrived to leave off just in the middle of a sentence, and in the nick of a story, where Tom Jones discovers Square behind the blanket; or where Parson Adams, in the inextricable confusion of events, very undesignedly gets to bed to Mrs. Slip-slop. . . .

I read a few poets, which did not much hit my taste—for I would have the reader understand, I am deficient in the faculty of imagination; but I fell early upon French romances and philosophy, and devoured them tooth-and-nail. Many a dainty repast have I made of the *New Eloise*;—the description of the kiss; the excursion on the water; the letter of St. Preux, recalling the time of their first loves; and the account of Julia's death; these I read over and over again with unspeakable delight and wonder. Some years after, when I met with this work again, I found I had lost nearly my whole relish for it (except some few parts), and was, I remember, very much mortified with the change in my taste, which I sought to attribute to the smallness and gilt edges of the edition I had bought, and its being perfumed with rose-leaves. . . .

Books have in a great measure lost their power over me; nor can I revive the same interest in them as formerly. I perceive when a thing is good, rather than feel it. It is true that the reading of Mr. Keats's *Eve of St. Agnes*

lately made me regret that I was not young again. The
beautiful and tender images there conjured up, "come
like shadows—so depart." The "tiger-moth's wings,"
which he has spread over his rich poetic blazonry, just
flit across my fancy; the gorgeous twilight window which
he has painted over again in his verse, to me "blushes"
almost in vain "with blood of queens and kings." I know
how I should have felt at one time in reading such passages; and that is all. The sharp luscious flavour, the fine
aroma is fled, and nothing but the stalk, the bran, the
husk of literature is left. If any one were to ask me what
I read now, I might answer with my Lord Hamlet in the
play—"Words, words, words."—"What is the
matter?"—"*Nothing!*"—They have scarce a meaning. But it was not always so. There was a time when to
my thinking, every word was a flower or a pearl, like
those which dropped from the mouth of the little peasant.
girl in the Fairy tale, or like those that fall from the
great preacher in the Caledonian Chapel! I drank of the
stream of knowledge that tempted, but did not mock my
lips, as of the river of life, freely. . . .

    I remember, as long ago as the year 1798, going to a
neighbouring town (Shrewsbury, where Farquhar has
laid the plot of his *Recruiting Officer*) and bringing
home with me, "at one proud swoop," a copy of Milton's
Paradise Lost, and another of Burke's *Reflections on
the French Revolution*—both which I have still; and
I still recollect, when I see the covers, the pleasure with
which I dipped into them as I returned with my double
prize. I was set up for one while. That time is past "with

all its giddy raptures:" but I am still anxious to preserve
its memory, "embalmed with odours". . . .

Whether those observations will survive me, I
neither know nor do I much care: but to the works themselves, "worthy of all acceptation," and to the feelings
they have always excited in me since I could distinguish
a meaning in language, nothing shall ever prevent me
from looking back with gratitude and triumph. To have
lived in the cultivation of an intimacy with such works,
and to have familiarly relished such names, is not to
have lived quite in vain. . . .

—1821

Library in the Timber

By STEWART H. HOLBROOK

HAD IT NOT BEEN FOR THE LIBRARY of Jackson Marks I should have found my first winter in a British Columbia logging camp less pleasant than it was. The camp was up the coast 300 miles from Vancouver, or anywhere else, and our connection with the outside world was one boat a week. The nights up there were very long, and so were the Sundays.

Jackson Marks was the saw-filer, and a man of parts to boot. Saws in that country come in narrow wooden boxes, 16 feet long. In his shack at camp Jackson had four of these boxes nailed along the walls. They were filled with books. Jackson went to town twice a year. First thing he did when he sighted electric lights and streetcars was to deposit $100 with a bookseller. He spent the rest of his stake, in the usual and quite care-free manner of lumberjacks, on booze, bawds and battle. But always, and first, $100 went for books, which he brought back to camp.

The Jackson Marks Library—and it deserved an uppercase "L"—was a godsend to the few literates in camp. It was here I first became acquainted with the sonorous periods of Gibbon. I read Carlyle that winter, and a good deal of Darwin and Huxley. But the range was catholic; I enjoyed Brann The Iconoclast, and

"Billy Baxter's Letters", written, I believe, for the bottlers of aperient water in the '90's. Jackson introduced me to "Tristram Shandy", to Voltaire, to Montaigne, and did his best to get me to wrestle with Euripides.

It was a great winter. Of an evening and on blustering Sundays, Jackson had me sit in his home-made flour-barrel rocker while he discoursed, in a scholarly manner well salted with lumberjack idiom, on what he termed The Curse of Harold Bell Wright. He urged me to read Volney's Ruins; he permitted but did not urge me to read his set of Wilkie Collins. ("I was drunk when I bought those", he explained.) He held that American biographical writing had improved but little since Parson Weems. He said a guy named Mencken was becoming the most powerful critical force in America. He opined that Colonel Ingersoll's lectures had freed the minds of Americans who now sought to discredit the gallant Colonel.

I never got around to go to college, but that one winter with Jackson himself, in the Jackson Marks Library—its kerosene lamp glowing yellow in the gloom of two-hundred-foot firs—was worth more to me, perhaps, than a year in a university, possibly two years.

—1939

My Books

By LEIGH HUNT

SITTING, LAST WINTER, among my books, and walled round with all the comfort and protection which they and my fireside could afford me; to wit, a table of high-piled books at my back, my writing-desk on one side of me, some shelves on the other, and the feeling of the warm fire at my feet; I began to consider how I loved the authors of those books —how I loved them, too, not only for the imaginative pleasures they afforded me, but for their making me love the very books themselves, and delight to be in contact with them. I looked sideways at my Spenser, my Theocritus, and my "Arabian Nights;" then above them at my Italian poets; then behind me at my Dryden and Pope, my romances, and my Boccaccio; then on my left side at my Chaucer, who lay on a writing-desk; and thought how natural it was in C.L. to give a kiss to an old folio, as I once saw him do to Chapman's Homer. Cooke's edition of the "British Poets and Novelists" came out when I was at school. Shall I ever forget his Collins and his Gray, books at once so "superbly ona-mented" and so inconceivably cheap? Sixpence could procure much before; but never could it procure so much as then, or was at once so much respected, and so little cared for. His artist Kirk was the best artist, except Stothard, that ever designed for periodical works. I shall never forget the gratitude with which I received an odd number of Akenside, value sixpence. It was the one in which there is a picture of the poet on a sofa, with Cupid coming to him, and the words underneath, "Tempt me no more, insidious love!" The picture and the number appeared to me equally divine. I cannot help thinking to this day, that it is right and natural in a gentleman to sit in a stage dress, on that particular kind of sofa, though on no other, with that exclusive hat and feathers on his head, telling Cupid to begone with a tragic air.

I love an author the more for having been himself a lover of books. Virgil must have been one; and, after a fashion, Martial. May I confess, that the passage which I recollect with the greatest pleasure in Cicero, is where he says that books delight us at home, *and are no impediment abroad;* travel with us, ruralize with us. His period is rounded off to some purpose: *"Delectant domi, non impediunt foris; peregrinantur, rusticantur."* I am so much of this opinion that I do not care to be anywhere without having a book or books at hand, and like Dr. Orkborne, in the novel of "Camilla," stuff the coach or post-chaise with them whenever I travel. Dante puts Homer, the great ancient, in his "Elysium" upon trust; but a few years afterwards, "Homer," the book, made its appearance in Italy, and Petrarch, in a transport, put it upon his bookshelves, where he adored it, like "the unknown God." Petrarch ought to be the god of the bibliomaniacs, for he was a collector and a man of genius, which is a union that does

not often happen. He copied out, with his own precious
hand, the manuscripts he rescued from time, and then
produced others for time to reverence. With his head
upon a book he died.

   Spenser's reading is evident by his learning; and if
there were nothing else to show for it in Shakspeare, his
retiring to his native town, long before old age, would be
a proof of it. It is impossible for a man to live in solitude
without such assistance, unless he is a metaphysician or
mathematician, or the dullest of mankind; and any
country town would be solitude to Shakspeare, after the
bustle of a metropolis and a theatre. Doubtless he
divided his time between his books, and his bowling-
green, and his daughter Susanna. It is pretty certain,
also, that he planted, and rode on horseback; and there
is evidence of all sorts to make it clear, that he must
have occasionally joked with the blacksmith, and stood
godfather for his neighbours' children.

   There will be something compulsory in reading the
"Ramblers," as there is in going to church. Gray was a
bookman; he wished to be always lying on sofas, reading
"eternal new novels of Crebillon and Marivaux."

   How pleasant it is to reflect, that all those lovers of
books have themselves become books! What better
metamorphosis could Pythagoras have desired? How
Ovid and Horace exulted in anticipating theirs! And how
the world have justified their exultation! They had a
right to triumph over brass and marble. It is the only
visible change which changes no farther; which generates
and yet is not destroyed. Consider: mines themselves are

exhausted; cities perish; kingdoms are swept away, and man weeps with indignation to think that his own body is not immortal.

Yet this little body of thought, that lies before me in the shape of a book, has existed thousands of years, nor since the invention of the press can anything short of an universal convulsion of nature abolish it. To a shape like this, so small yet so comprehensive, so slight yet so lasting, so insignificant yet so venerable, turns the mighty activity of Homer, and so turning, is enabled to live and warm us for ever. To a shape like this turns the placid sage of Academus: to a shape like this the grandeur of Milton, the exuberance of Spenser, the pungent elegance of Pope, and the volatility of Prior. In one small room, like the compressed spirits of Milton, can be gathered together

The assembled souls of all that men held wise.

May I hope to become the meanest of these existences? This is a question which every author who is a lover of books asks himself some time in his life; and which must be pardoned, because it cannot be helped. I know not. But I should like to remain visible in this shape. The little of myself that pleases myself, I could wish to be accounted worth pleasing others. I should like to survive so, were it only for the sake of those who love me in private, knowing as I do what a treasure is the possession of a friend's mind when he is no more. At all events, nothing while I live and think can deprive me of my value for such treasures. I can help the appreciation of them while I last, and love them till I die; and perhaps, if fortune turns her face once more in kindness upon me before I go, I may chance, some quiet day, to lay my overbeating temples on a book, and so have the death I most envy.

—1823

Conversations With Kafka

By GUSTAV JANOUCH

A FEW DAYS LATER I MET KAFKA by arrangement at five o'clock in the evening outside his father's warehouse. We intended to take a walk on the Hradschin. But Kafka was not well. He breathed with difficulty. So we merely strolled across the Altstadter Ring, past the Niklas Church in the Karpfengasse and by way of the Rathaus to the Kleine Ring. We stopped outside Calve's bookshop and looked into the windows.

I bent my head to right and left, trying to read the titles on the backs of the books. Kafka was amused, and laughed.

'So you too are a lunatic about books, with a head that wags from too much reading?'

'That's right. I don't think I could exist without books. To me, they're the whole world.'

Kafka's eyebrows narrowed.

'That's a mistake. A book cannot take the place of the world. That is impossible. In life, everything has its own meaning and its own purpose, for which there cannot be any permanent substitute. A man can't, for instance, master his own experience through the medium of another personality. That is how the world is in relation to books. One tries to imprison life in a book, like a songbird in a cage, but it's no good. On the contrary!

Out of the abstractions one finds in books, one can only construct systems that are cages for oneself. Philosophers are only brightly clad Papagenos with their own different cages.'

He laughed. This was followed by a hollow, ugly cough. When the attack was over, he said with a smile: 'I have told the truth. You have just heard it and seen it. What other people do through the nose, I have to say with my lungs.' This gave me an unpleasant feeling. To repress it, I said: 'Have you caught cold? Haven't you got a temperature?'

Kafka gave a tired smile: 'No . . . I'm never warm enough. So I am always burning . . . from cold.'

He wiped the sweat from his forehead with his handkerchief. His tight-pressed lips were framed by two deeply cut lines at the corners of his mouth.

He held out his hand.

'Goodbye.'

I could find nothing to say.

I surprised Franz Kafka in his office studying a catalogue of the *Reclam-Bucherei*.

'I am getting drunk on book titles,' said Kafka. 'Books are a narcotic.'

I opened my brief-case and showed him the contents.

'I am a hashish addict, Herr Doktor.'

Kafka was amazed.

'Nothing but new books!'

I emptied the brief-case on to his writing-desk. Kafka took one book after the other, turned the pages, read a passage here and there, and returned me the book.

'And you are going to read all that?'

I nodded.

Kafka pursed his lips.

'You spend too much time on ephemeras. The majority of modern books are merely wavering reflections of the present. They disappear very quickly. You should read more old books. The classics. Goethe. What is old reveals its deepest value—lastingness. What is merely new is the most transitory of all things. It is beautiful today, and tomorrow merely ludicrous. That is the way of literature.'

'And poetry?'

'Poetry transforms life. Sometimes that is even worse.'

A knock at the door. Enter my father.

'Is my son and heir being a nuisance?'

Kafka smiled.

'Oh, no! We are discussing devils and demons.'

—1921

An Autolycus of the Bookstalls

By WALTER JERROLD

IT HAS SOMETIMES SEEMED TO ME that the owners of the "proud libraries" which Walt Whitman begged should not be shut against his poems know nothing of the keenest pleasure that comes to the book-lover among his books. As one who has long been an Autolycus of the bookstalls, a snapper-up of unconsidered trifles from the twopenny box, I can say that among the finest delights of book acquisition has been the aimless hunting with which I have turned over the piled-up treasures of the bookstalls, either ranged along the kerbstone in the poorer districts, or among the gregarious stores of old Booksellers' Row (call it not Holywell Street!) and of that newer Booksellers' Row which has sprung up in Charing Cross Road.

There is, no doubt, a real delight in book-hunting as the term is generally understood, in having a "subject," and seeking everywhere for anything bearing in any way upon it. The instinct of the hunting animal is brought into play and diverted—the seeker after big game, instead of tracking the tiger in the jungles of Bengal, or the grizzly in his fastnesses in the Rockies, hunts, say, Aldines and Elzevirs in the highways and byeways where civilised men most do congregate. Such find a pleasure in their chase, no doubt, and are acquainted with the keen thrill of satisfaction which attends the acquisition of a rarity, but greater, as it seems to me, is the delight of Autolycus; with a ready appreciation of a hundred subjects, with a taste most catholic, he finds his pleasure in every street that boasts a bookshop; he is liker to your poet than to your hunter, finding inspiration in surroundings seemingly most adverse. Such an Autolycus—I may speak, I hope, as one of a large family, numbering Charles Lamb among the most glorious of its ancestors—could not always render a reason for the purchase of a certain book, any more than the poet could explain to the understanding of the Utilitarian why it was that he paused to drink in the beauty of the flower which arrested his attention.

Standing among my books after some twenty years of Autolycusising, and glancing over the ever-growing shelves, I am struck by the way in which such a collection is divisible into four or five sharply-defined classes, according to the manner in which they have been acquired. The books bought as mood, governed by price, has dictated during long hauntings of metropolitan bookstalls form a class by themselves; secondly, there are the presentation copies from author-friends; next come the copies obtained during some years as reviewer of miscellaneous literature; and then those books-which-are-no-books—as Lamb happily expressed it—the mere tools of the literary craftsman in works of reference, guides, annuals, *et hoc genus omne*. Such classification is, of course, not final; it does not allow for inevitable overlappings. There *are* presentation copies which we might have obtained by purchase *if we had not known the authors thereof*; there *are* works of reference that deservedly rank with literature and not with Elia's *biblia abiblia*—the "Encyclopedia Britannica," to wit. Still, broadly speaking, the classification holds good, and of all the groups that which is to me the most attractive is the first. It is—I hope that my author-friends will not cut me off with review copies for the confession—as a whole even more attractive than the presentation group, rich as that is in intimate personal associations. "A book's a book although there's nothing in't," wrote a poet who gave us many volumes of a more positive sort; a book is never as much a book, I would say, as when a sacrifice has been made to obtain it. Some of the volumes dearest to Autolycus are assuredly those to the purchase of which went a part—sometimes the greater part—of his "dinner-money" in his clerk-ship days. Pleasant, indeed, were those noon hours spent in Booksellers' Row—with an occasional excursion to Farringdon Street, Aldgate, or the New Cut—bright oases in the day's journeyings through deserts of arid figures; and glorious, indeed, were the modest biblical "finds" obtainable at so slight a sacrifice.

Musing on these old purchases, I have glanced here and there over my shelves, picking out friends first made in days that would be dull indeed in memory but for these associations. Here is the Cromwellian "Flagellum" of Carlyle's "poor Carrion" Heath, with additions by Grangerising and marginalia-writing owners of pronounced Royalist proclivities, picked up for a few pence

from a wayside barrow. Here is a sixteen-page autobiography of William Cobbett, published in 1816 for four-
pence, and warranted on the title-page to contain "as
much as a half-crown pamphlet"—picked up for a
penny a few years ago from an *olla podrida* of ephem-
eral literature. Here is a copy of the second edition of
"An Essay on Criticism," written by Mr Pope, for
which was paid the same insignificant sum of one penny.
Small sacrifices these, even for Autolycus when most
impecunious. One of his earliest purchases was a single
volume small-type reprint of Pope's works, obtained
to satisfy a boyish wish—fired by quotations—to read
the "Iliad" in its entirety; as the boy Cobbett had
sacrificed a meal for "The Tale of a Tub," he did the
same in unconscious imitation for Pope's "Poetical
Works." That poor tattered paper-covered volume
has gone I know not whither, for in happy hour its
possessor lighted upon the entire works of Pope, in
fifteen volumes, whole calf, unstained, and as fresh as
though they had remained unopened in some proud
library—too proud for use!—since they were printed in
1770. The whole fifteen volumes were willingly handed
over by the dealer in exchange for three shillings and
sixpence. Pence, and but a few in the pocket at a time
have, however, sufficed to add incalculable wealth to
the store.

At various times, and at various places, at prices
ranging from twopence to as many shillings, have been
obtained friends that are such for all time. Here are
"The Essays or Counsels, Civil and Moral, of Sir Francis

Bacon, Lord Verulam, Viscount St Alban, with a Table
of the Colours of Good and Evil. Whereunto is added the
Wisdom of the Ancients. Enlarged by the Honorable
Author himself; and now more exactly Published"
(1673). The title-page, with its triple insistence upon
the personality of the "honourable author," should
afford a nice reproof for those inexact persons, who,
following Macaulay and other authorities, *will* speak
of Lord Bacon. The next book I take down gives me
pause, for surely nothing short of a love for everything
bearing the name of the author of "The Vicar of Wakefield" could have dictated the purchase of "Poems for
Young Ladies. In Three Parts: Devotional, Moral, and
Entertaining. The Whole being a Collection of the Best
Pieces in our Language. By Dr Goldsmith." It throws
a curious light upon the literary taste of the time to
find that Goldsmith borrowed from "Paradise Lost"
without acknowledgment; Mr Pope, Mr Prior, Dr
Parnell, Mr Collins, etc., were evidently names to
conjure with, but "Mr Anon" seems to have been
better appreciated than Mr Milton, and that despite
Addison's eulogy of half-a-century earlier. It is strange
to find that all "the best pieces in our language" were
written between the days of Edmund Waller and those
of Collins! Another time, for the price of one penny—
the monetary standard always becomes especially
ridiculous when applied to literature,—was picked up
the two volumes in one of *The North Briton* (1784)
in which John Wilkes made his sustained and caustic
attack on Lord Bute; double that sum bought the

volume of *The Freeholder* (1716), Addison's single-handed successor to *The Spectator.*

Southey, whose genius is nowadays more or less under a cloud of neglect, has provided Autolycus with two "finds," in which he takes perennial delight; of neither of them would he have known anything had he not snapped them up from the seemingly dingy treasure-houses which he haunts. One is a massive volume of upwards of a thousand pages—a stinging commentary on poor Goldsmith's conventional "Best Pieces"—and it is entitled "Select Works of the British Poets from Chaucer to Jonson, with Biographical Sketches by Robert Southey, Esq., L.L.D." Issued by Longmans in 1831, this is one of the richest single volumes in existence—rich not only in generally accepted poetical treasure which may be obtained in a dozen editions, but also in works not easy to secure. Within its covers are to be found Tusser's "Five Hundred Points of Good Husbandry." Skelton's "Colyn Clout," and "Philip Sparow," Hawes' "Pastime of Plesure," Drayton's "Poly-olbion" (in its entirety!), Phineas Fletcher's "Purple Island," and his brother's sacred poems, Habington's "Castara," etc. These are but some of the least easily obtainable works included in this biblical gold-mine (to use a simile appreciable by a commercial-minded folk). There are besides—again to name only a selection—the whole of "The Faerie Queene," and poems by Donne, Withers, Lovelace, Drummond, Carew, Fulke Greville, Gascoigne, etc. Compelled to limit himself to the reading of one book, what lover of poetry would not unhesitatingly decide upon this library in a single volume? The other work of Southey's for which Autolycus feels a strong regard is "The Doctor," the first five volumes of which, published anonymously during the author's lifetime, were picked up a few years ago for half-a-crown. This strange medley, charged with all manner of learning, yet never loaded with it, is one of the most delightful of works in that class of what might be called inconsequent books—books in which the author gossips on wisely, profoundly, humorously, by turns, on all manner of subjects as they arise. For the sake of those poor folk—Autolycus pities them from the bottom of his heart—who read none but new books, or old books new-issued, it is to be wished that some enterprising publisher would give us a fresh edition of the fascinating "Doctor," acquaintance with whom is at once a source of much entertainment and a liberal education in Literature.

It is impossible to bring within the purview of a single chapter all the fruits gathered from the bookstalls, and I have named but one or two "finds" that have been taken more or less at haphazard from the shelves. They serve to show that to-day, as in the days of Dibdin, the second-hand bookshops yet have in them something better than tattered copies of the dominant novel, either in its superseded three-volume form, or in the paper covers of its latest manifestation. There are other pleasures of the Autolycus of the bookstalls which might be mentioned. There is an unquestionable delight in buying an odd volume and haunting the stalls in a search for its companions. For a single penny, some eighteen years ago, I purchased Tennyson's "Queen Mary," in the neat red cloth "Cabinet edition." Thenceforth, there was, besides the general pleasure of turning over the bookstall wares, the delight of occasionally picking up a fresh volume of the series, until gradually—it took about ten years—the set of fourteen volumes was completed. Another "hunt" of the same kind has been for the original issues of the pocketable volumes of the companionable Bayard Series—a hunt which still gives pleasure, for there is the hope that some day with that luck which attends Autolycus upon his wanderings he may add Mr Swinburne's "Coleridge's Christabel, and other Imaginative Poems" to its many-coloured companions. Then, too, there is the joy which comes when lighting upon the unique in unexpected places—as when on "picking up" a copy of Bentham's "Fragment on Government" it was found to be enriched with the autograph of Cardinal Manning. The pleasures of the Bookstall Autolycus are manifold, and though the days when he could acquire rare folios for a few shillings have gone or become as rare as angels' visits, yet is there a perennial delight in snapping up such unconsidered trifles as those of which a few are here indicated.

—1902

Detached Thoughts on Books and Reading

By CHARLES LAMB

*To mind the inside of a book is to
entertain one's self with the forced
product of another man's brain.
Now I think a man of quality and
breeding may be much amused
with the natural sprouts of his own.*
—Lord Foppington in the Relapse

AN INGENIOUS ACQUAINTANCE of my own
was so much struck with this bright sally of his
Lordship, that he has left off reading altogether,
to the great improvement of his originality. At
the hazard of losing some credit on this head, I must
confess that I dedicate no inconsiderable portion of my
time to other people's thoughts. I dream away my life
in others' speculations. I love to lose myself in other
men's minds. When I am not walking, I am reading; I
cannot sit and think. Books think for me.

I have no repugnances. Shaftesbury is not too
genteel for me, nor Jonathan Wild too low. I can read
anything which I call a *book*. There are things in that
shape which I cannot allow for such.

In this catalogue of *books which are no books—
biblia abiblia*—I reckon Court Calendars, Directories,
Pocket Books, Draught Boards, bound and lettered on

the back, Scientific Treatises, Almanacks, Statutes at
Large; the works of Hume, Gibbon, Robertson, Beattie,
Soame Jenyns, and, generally, all those volumes which
"no gentleman's library should be without": the
Histories of Flavius Josephus (that learned Jew), and
Paley's Moral Philosophy. With these exceptions, I
can read almost anything. I bless my stars for a taste
so catholic, so unexcluding.

I confess that it moves my spleen to see these
things in books' clothing perched upon shelves,
like false saints, usurpers of true shrines, intruders
into the sanctuary, thrusting out the legitimate
occupants. To reach down a well-bound semblance
of a volume, and hope it some kind-hearted play-
book, then, opening what "seem its leaves," to
come bolt upon a withering Population Essay. To
expect a Steele, or a Farquhar, and find—Adam
Smith. To view a well-arranged assortment of block-
headed Encyclopedias (Anglicanas or Metropoli-
tanas) set out in an array of Russia, or Morocco,
when a tithe of that good leather would comfortably
re-clothe my shivering folios; would renovate Para-
celsus himself, and enable old Raymund Lully to
look like himself again in the world. I never see
these impostors, but I long to strip them, to warm
my ragged veterans in their spoils.

To be strong-backed and neat-bound is the
desideratum of a volume. Magnificence comes
after. This, when it can be afforded, is not to be
lavished upon all kinds of books indiscriminately.

I would not dress a set of Magazines, for instance, in full suit. The dishabille, or half-binding (with Russia backs ever) is *our* costume. A Shakspeare, or a Milton (unless the first editions), it were mere foppery to trick out in gay apparel. The possession of them confers no distinction. The exterior of them (the things themselves being so common), strange to say, raises no sweet emotions, no tickling sense of property in the owner. Thomson's Seasons, again, looks best (I maintain it) a little torn, and dog's-eared. How beautiful to a genuine lover of reading are the sullied leaves, and worn-out appearance, nay, the very odour (beyond Russia), if we would not forget kind feelings in fastidiousness, of an old "Circulating Library" Tom Jones, or Vicar of Wakefield! How they speak of the thousand thumbs, that have turned over their pages with delight!—of the lone semp-stress, whom they may have cheered (milliner, or hard-working mantua-maker) after her long day's needle-toil, running far into midnight, when she has snatched an hour, ill-spared from sleep, to steep her cares, as in some Lethean cup, in spelling out their enchanting contents! Who would have them a whit less soiled? What better condition could we desire to see them in?

In some respects the better a book is, the less it demands from binding. Fielding, Smollet, Sterne, and all that class of perpetually self-reproductive volumes—Great Nature's Stereotypes— we see them individually perish with less regret, because we know the copies of them to be "eterne." But where a book

is at once both good and rare—where the individual
is almost the species, and when *that* perishes,

> We know not where is that Promethean torch
> That can its light relumine—

such a book, for instance, as the Life of the Duke of
Newcastle, by his Duchess—no casket is rich enough, no
casing sufficiently durable, to honour and keep safe such
a jewel.

Not only rare volumes of this description, which seem
hopeless ever to be reprinted; but old editions of writers,
such as Sir Philip Sydney, Bishop Taylor, Milton in his
prose-works, Fuller—of whom we *have* reprints, yet
the books themselves, though they go about, and are
talked of here and there, we know, have not endenizened
themselves (nor possibly ever will) in the national heart,
so as to become stock books—it is good to possess these
in durable and costly covers. I do not care for a First
Folio of Shakspeare. I rather prefer the common
editions of Rowe and Tonson without notes, and with
plates, which, being so execrably bad, serve as maps,
or modest remembrancers, to the text; and without
pretending to any supposable emulation with it, are
so much better than the Shakspeare gallery *engravings*, which *did*. I have a community of feeling
with my countrymen about his Plays, and I like
those editions of him best, which have been oftenest
tumbled about and handled.—On the contrary, I
cannot read Beaumont and Fletcher but in Folio.
The Octavo editions are painful to look at. I have no

sympathy with them. If they were as much read as the current editions of the other poet, I should prefer them in that shape to the older one. I do not know a more heartless sight than the reprint of the Anatomy of Melancholy. What need was there of unearthing the bones of that fantastic old great man, to expose them in a winding-sheet of the newest fashion to modern censure? what hapless stationer could dream of Burton ever becoming popular?—The wretched Malone could not do worse, when he bribed the sexton of Stratford church to let him white-wash the painted effigy of old Shakspeare, which stood there, in rude but lively fashion depicted, to the very colour of the cheek, the eye, the eyebrow, hair, the very dress he used to wear—the only authentic testimony we had, however imperfect, of these curious parts and parcels of him. They covered him over with a coat of white paint. By——, if I had been a justice of peace for Warwickshire, I would have clapt both commentator and sexton fast in the stocks, for a pair of meddling sacrilegious varlets.

I think I see them at their work—these sapient trouble-tombs.

Shall I be thought fantastical, if I confess, that the names of some of our poets sound sweeter, and have a finer relish to the ear—to mine, at least— than that of Milton or of Shakspeare? It may be, that the latter are more staled and rung upon in common discourse. The sweetest names, and which carry a perfume in the mention, are, Kit Marlowe,

Drayton, Drummond of Hawthornden, and Cowley.

Much depends upon *when* and *where* you read a book. In the five or six impatient minutes, before the dinner is quite ready, who would think of taking up the Fairy Queen for a stop-gap, or a volume of Bishop Andrewes' sermons?

Milton almost requires a solemn service of music to be played before you enter upon him. But he brings his music, to which, who listens, had need bring docile thoughts, and purged ears.

Winter evenings—the world shut out—with less of ceremony the gentle Shakspeare enters. At such a season, the Tempest, or his own Winter's Tale—

These two poets you cannot avoid reading aloud —to yourself, or (as it chances) to some single person listening. More than one—and it degenerates into an audience.

Books of quick interest, that hurry on for incidents, are for the eye to glide over only. It will not do to read them out. I could never listen to even the better kind of modern novels without extreme irk-someness. . . .

I am not much a friend to out-of-doors reading. I cannot settle my spirits to it. I knew a Unitarian minister, who was generally to be seen upon Snow Hill (as yet Skinner's Street *was not*), between the hours of ten and eleven in the morning, studying a volume of Lardner. I own this to have been a strain of abstraction beyond my reach. I used to admire how he sidled along, keeping clear of secular contacts.

An illiterate encounter with a porter's knot, or a
bread basket, would have quickly put to flight all the
theology I am master of, and have left me worse
than indifferent to the five points.

There is a class of street-readers, whom I can
never contemplate without affection—the poor
gentry, who, not having wherewithal to buy or hire
a book, filch a little learning at the open stalls—the
owner, with his hard eye, casting envious looks at
them all the while, and thinking when they will have
done. Venturing tenderly, page after page, expecting
every moment when he shall interpose his interdict,
and yet unable to deny themselves the gratification,
they "snatch a fearful joy." Martin Burney, in this
way, by daily fragments, got through two volumes of
Clarissa, when the stall-keeper damped his laudable
ambition, by asking him (it was in his younger
days) whether he meant to purchase the work. M.
declares, that under no circumstance in his life
did he ever peruse a book with half the satisfaction
which he took in those uneasy snatches. . . .

—1822

The Autobiography of Malcolm X

By *MALCOLM X* & *ALEX HALEY*

I SAW THAT THE BEST THING I could do was get hold of a dictionary—to study, to learn some words. I was lucky enough to reason also that I should try to improve my penmanship. It was sad. I couldn't even write in a straight line. It was both ideas together that moved me to request a dictionary along with some tablets and pencils from the Norfolk Prison Colony school.

I spent two days just riffling uncertainly through the dictionary's pages. I'd never realized so many words existed! I didn't know *which* words I needed to learn. Finally, just to start some kind of action, I began copying.

In my slow, painstaking, ragged handwriting, I copied into my tablet everything printed on that first page, down to the punctuation marks.

I believe it took me a day. Then, aloud, I read back, to myself, everything I'd written on the tablet. Over and over, aloud, to myself, I read my own handwriting.

I woke up the next morning, thinking about those words—immensely proud to realize that not only had I written so much at one time, but I'd written words that I never knew were in the world. Moreover, with a little effort, I also could remember what many of these words meant. I reviewed the words whose meanings I didn't remember. Funny thing, from the dictionary first page right now, that "aardvark" springs to my mind. The dictionary had a picture of it, a long-tailed, long-eared, burrowing African mammal, which lives off termites caught by sticking out its tongue as an anteater does for ants.

I was so fascinated that I went on—I copied the dictionary's next page. And the same experience came when I studied that. With every succeeding page, I also learned of people and places and events from history. Actually the dictionary is like a miniature encyclopedia. Finally the dictionary's A section had filled a whole tablet—and I went on into the B's. That was the way I started copying what eventually became the entire dictionary. It went a lot faster after so much practice helped me to pick up hand-writing speed. Between what I wrote in my tablet, and writing letters, during the rest of my time in prison I would guess I wrote a million words.

I suppose it was inevitable that as my word-base broadened, I could for the first time pick up a book and read and now begin to understand what the book was saying. Anyone who has read a great deal can imagine the new world that opened. Let me tell you something: from then until I left that prison, in every free moment I had, if I was not reading in the library, I was reading on my bunk. You couldn't have gotten me out of books with a wedge. Between Mr. Muhammad's teachings, my correspondence, my visitors—usually Ella and Reginald—and my reading of books, months passed without my even thinking about being imprisoned. In fact, up to then, I never had been so truly free in my life.

The Norfolk Prison Colony's library was in the school building. A variety of classes was taught there by instructors who came from such places as Harvard and Boston universities. The weekly debates between inmate teams were also held in the school building. You would be astonished to know how worked up convict debaters and audiences would get over subjects like "Should Babies Be Fed Milk?"

Available on the prison library's shelves were books on just about every general subject. Much of the big private collection that Parkhurst had willed to the prison was still in crates and boxes in the back of the library—thousands of old books. Some of them looked ancient: covers faded, old-time parchment-looking binding. Parkhurst, I've mentioned, seemed to have been principally interested in history and religion. He had the money and the special interest to have a lot of books that you wouldn't have in general circulation. Any college library would have been lucky to get that collection.

As you can imagine, especially in a prison where there was heavy emphasis on rehabilitation, an inmate was smiled upon if he demonstrated an unusually intense interest in books. There was a sizable number of well-read inmates, especially the popular debaters. Some were said by many to be practically walking encyclopedias. They were almost celebrities. No university would ask any student to devour literature as I did when this new world opened to me, of being able to read and *understand*.

I read more in my room than in the library itself. An inmate who was known to read a lot could check out more than the permitted maximum number of books. I preferred reading in the total isolation of my own room.

When I had progressed to really serious reading, every night at about ten P.M. I would be outraged with the "lights out." It always seemed to catch me right in the middle of something engrossing.

Fortunately, right outside my door was a corridor light that cast a glow into my room. The glow was enough to read by, once my eyes adjusted to it. So when "lights out" came, I would sit on the floor where I could continue reading in that glow.

At one-hour intervals the night guards paced past every room. Each time I heard the approaching footsteps, I jumped into bed and feigned sleep. And as soon as the guard passed, I got back out of bed onto the floor area of that light-glow, where I would read for another fifty-eight minutes—until the guard approached again. That went on until three or four every morning. Three or four hours of sleep a night was enough for me. Often in the years in the streets I had slept less than that.

—1964

Bookstore Bargains

By JIM McGINN

I FEAR I MAY actually get more pleasure from many a book's purchase than its perusal. That explains why my collection of unread books continues to grow while my appetite for expanding that mass never seems to wane. No matter how many times I resolve not to buy another book until I have read at least two of the previous purchases, things never seem to work out as planned.

Actually, I know what lies behind my proclivity for buying paperbacks—a great bargain. The other day is a case in point. 20 books for a grand total of $7.20. Count 'em, 20. This heist took place at Marty's, a small shop in Revere—on Boston's North Shore—just down from Bell Circle heading north on American Legion Highway, diagonally across from Blanchard's supermarket. My financial advisor informed me that averaged out to 36 cents a book, which distressed me only slightly. On my first trip to Marty's, last fall, I walked away with 12 books for only $4.20, a 35 cent norm. Ah, the ravages of inflation.

You can surely appreciate my satisfaction at these 35-36 cent buys when I confess that over the past 12 years I have been paying almost twice that amount for books. Of course, my shopping M.O. is certainly not everyone's. And I am primarily interested in fiction. It appeals to me as being more realistic than most non-fiction, though I admit to not having read Geraldo's autobiography or a Kitty Kelley masterpiece. The first time I stopped at Marty's, who also stocks aspirin, toothbrushes, crayons and electrical tape for sale by his register, 11 of the 12 books I came away with were fiction, the twelfth being Leo Damore's *Senatorial Privilege, the Chappaquiddick Cover-up.* (Come to think of it, any book relating to Teddy Kennedy's version of events at Chappaquiddick, might well qualify as a work of fiction also.)

Acquiring such inexpensive jewels for me is, I imagine, like a K-Mart customer hearing the following announcement: "Attention K-Mart shoppers! All men's $35 blue jeans and slacks are now on sale for 99 cents." Or an equally astonishing proclamation at Purity Supreme supermarket: "Our one gallon containers of milk are now selling for 4 cents." Utterly ridiculous you say. As for the K-Mart and Purity scenarios, correct, but how else is one to regard purchasing *Centennial* (1,082pp.), *The Talisman* (768pp.) and *Don Quixote* (432pp.) in exchange for only one George Washington?

Books are not something I buy so much as hunt. Now, one may travel another path to acquire a book, as I have done myself on occasion, by visiting a spotless, antiseptic looking bookstore. Yet, I find it pre-

ferable to go the first route, which at times
assumes the nature of an archeological dig. The
voyage by way of visiting those sidestreet shops
such as Marty's, is more cluttered and time-
consuming, but it always holds out more promise
of unearthing true treasure. After nearly two hours
of combing through Marty's 5,000 books the other
day, I did, indeed, discover gold—*The Story of
Henri Tod*, by William F. Buckley.

I had owned and read *Henri Tod* years previously. With the exception of *Stained Glass*, it
was my favorite in Buckley's Blackford Oakes spy
series and the only one in the series missing from
my collection. Peculiar how I have read all nine
novels in the series, enjoyed them all, yet these two,
Stained Glass and *The Story of Henri Tod*,
each have that mysterious ingredient which makes
certain books a life experience while others are
better classified as pleasant diversions. Over the
years, while tirelessly sifting like a Gold Rush
prospector through various shops, it had always
been in the recesses of my mind that *Henri Tod*
might someday, when I least expected it, reappear.

Why didn't I just visit a Barnes & Noble and
just lift the book off a shelf? Fair question. First,
my intention was to possess the book, to have it
occupy an honored spot on my bookshelf where
only a select number of my "Hall-of-Fame" books
are allowed to reside, not necessarily to reread it.
Second, and most important, is the enjoyment of

the hunt itself and its seldom equalled satisfaction
of finding a sought-after favorite title or a total
"stranger" which eventually evolves into a life-
long cherished "friend."

My exclusive Hall-of-Fame numbers less than
20. It is quite a motley collection ranging from
the beautiful hardcover edition—obviously, a gift
to me—of James McPherson's terrific *Battle Cry
of Freedom* to another Civil War work, Michael
Shaara's account of the battle of Gettysburg, *The
Killer Angels*, in a frayed, coverless, paperback
edition. A book can enter my Hall-of-Fame in one
of two ways. First, it can be like one of those life
experience reads I previously mentioned—a
Stained Glass, an *Atlas Shrugged*, a *To Kill a
Mockingbird*, or a *Studs Lonigan* fit into this
category. Each of those books contained such
memorable, invaluable lessons on life and left such
indelible impressions upon me that we—the books
and I—are permanently linked. The only other way
for a book to qualify for my shrine is to be an
absolutely great read; a fun or emotionally engrossing read whose ending brings not the satisfaction
of a task completed, but more an emptiness for the
loss of something dear. Joseph Heller's *Catch 22*;
Larry McMurtry's *Lonesome Dove*; Heywood
Gould's *Fort Apache, The Bronx*; Philip Rosen-
berg's *Contract on Cherry Street*; and Herbert
Kastle's *Death Squad* are all great reads.

Given my predilection for coverless paper-

backs, I have often wondered where these coverless
editions emanate from, and why no covers. But
beyond this, and being grateful for their availability, I have never given it much further thought.
Not until recently that is, when I picked up a
little biography of Michael Landon that I was
certain someone I knew would enjoy. Sure enough,
she did. What's more, she made a point the next
time she saw me of thanking me for the "stolen
property" I had obtained for her. It seems that
on one of the front pages of the book was the
printed warning:

> *If you purchase this book without a
> cover, you should be aware that this
> book is stolen property. It was
> reported as "unsold and destroyed"
> to the publisher and neither the
> author nor the publisher has received
> any payment for this "stripped book."*

I immediately experienced the panicky
thought that those hundreds of proud "steals" I
had obtained over the years were actually "stolen"
steals. With trepidation I began to check through
my sans-cover Hall-of-Famers like *Contract on
Cherry Street* and *Fort Apache, The Bronx*, to
my relief I found no such hot book warnings on
them. So while I do not intend to turn myself over
to Federal authorities for the Michael Landon
book, I will be more cognizant of that warning in

the future. An unconscionable discount is one thing, but I draw the line at theft.

It is a good thing I do not have an analyst. How would I ever explain to her the dichotomy of my being in favor of capital punishment while at the same instant being utterly incapable of throwing away a book, no matter how unenjoyable I found it. Certain crimes and criminals do not rate a second chance with me, while I always have hope that a book, however undistinguished in my eyes, will perhaps at another time, paroled to another state, find an appreciative reader.

As for my Hall-of-Fame books, I have one simple wish for those whose paper outlasts my flesh, may they go to someone—like the editor of this piece—who understands what a terrific impact, thrill and experience a book can mean, or be, to a person; someone who would make the effort to distribute my priceless treasures (currently estimated as being worth in excess of $40, but probably not more than $50) to other readers who might, by chance, profit in gaining one-half the pleasure from them that I did.

—1993

The Books in My Life

By HENRY MILLER

IN THE APPENDIX the reader will find a list of authors and titles arranged in a frank and curious way. I mention it because I think it important to stress at the outset a psychological fact about the reading of books which is rather neglected in most works on the subject. It is this: many of the books one lives with in one's mind are books one has never read. Sometimes these take on amazing importance. There are at least three categories of this order. The first comprises those books which one has every intention of reading some day but in all probability never will; the second comprises those books which one feels he ought to have read, and which, some at least, he undoubtedly will read before he dies; the third comprises the books one hears about, talks about, reads about, but which one is almost certain never to read because nothing, seemingly, can ever break down the wall of prejudice erected against them.

In the first category are those monumental works, classics mostly, which one is usually ashamed to admit he has never read: tomes one nibbles at occasionally, only to push them away, more than ever convinced that they are still unreadable. The list varies with the individual. For myself, to give a few outstanding names, they comprise the works of such celebrated authors as Homer, Aristotle, Francis Bacon, Hegel, Rousseau (excepting *Emile*), Robert Browning, Santayana. In the second category I include *Arabia Deserta*, the *Decline and Fall of the Roman Empire*, *The Hundred and Twenty Days of Sodom*, Casanova's *Memoirs*, Napoleon's *Memoirs*, Michelet's *History of the French Revolution*. In the third Pepys' *Diary*, *Tristram Shandy*, *Wilhelm Meister*, *The Anatomy of Melancholy*, *The Red and the Black*, *Marius the Epicurean*, *The Education of Henry Adams*.

Sometimes a chance reference to an author one has neglected to read or abandoned all thought of ever reading—a passage, say, in the work of an author one admires, or the words of a friend who is also a book lover—is sufficient to make one run for a book, read it with new eyes and claim it as one's very own. In the main, however, the books one neglects, or deliberately spurns, seldom get read. Certain subjects, certain styles, or unfortunate associations connected with the very names of certain books, create a repugnance almost insuperable. Nothing on earth, for example, could induce me to tackle anew Spenser's *Faery Queen*, which I began in college and fortunately dropped because I left that institution in a hurry. Never again will I look at a line of Edmund Burke, or Addison, or Chaucer, though the last-named I think altogether worthy of reading. Racine and Corneille are two others I doubt if I shall ever

look at again, though Corneille intrigues me because
of a brilliant essay I read not long ago on *Phedre* in
The Clown's Grail. On the other hand there are
books which lie at the very foundations of literature
but which are so remote from one's thinking and
experience as to render them "untouchable." Certain
authors, supposed to be the bulwark of our particular Western culture, are more foreign in spirit to me
than are the Chinese, the Arabs, or primitive
peoples. Some of the most exciting literary works
spring from cultures which have not contributed
directly to our development. No fairy tales, for
example, have exercised a more potent influence over
me than those of the Japanese, which I became
acquainted with through the work of Lafcadio Hearn,
one of the exotic figures in American literature. No
stories were more seductive to me as a child than
those drawn from the *Arabian Nights' Entertainment*. American Indian folklore leaves me cold,
whereas the folklore of Africa is near and dear to me.
And, as I have said repeatedly, whatever I read of
Chinese literature (barring Confucius) seems as if
written by my immediate ancestors.

I said that sometimes it is an esteemed author
who puts one on the track of a buried book. "What!
He liked *that* book?" you say to yourself, and
immediately the barriers fall away and the mind
becomes not only open and receptive but positively
aflame. Often it happens that it is not a friend of
similar tastes who revives one's interest in a dead

book but a chance acquaintance. Sometimes this
individual gives the impression of being a nitwit, and
one wonders why he should retain the memory of a
book which this person casually recommended, or
perhaps did not recommend at all but merely mentioned in the course of conversation as being an
"odd" book. In a vacant mood, at loose ends, as we
say, suddenly the recollection of this conversation
occurs, and we are ready to give the book a trial.
Then comes a shock, the shock of discovery. *Wuth-
ering Heights* is for me an example of this sort.
From having heard it praised so much and so often,
I had concluded that it was impossibe for an English
novel—by a woman!—to be that good. Then one day
a friend, whose taste I suspected to be shallow, let
drop a few pregnant words about it. Though I
promptly proceeded to forget his remarks, the poison
sank into me. Without realizing it, I nurtured a
secret resolve to have a look at this famous book one
day. Finally, just a few years ago, Jean Varda put it
in my hands. I read it in one gulp, astounded as is
everyone, I suspect, by its amazing power and
beauty. Yes, one of the very great novels in the
English language. And I, through pride and prejudice, had almost missed reading it.

—1969

Through My Guide-Books

By JAN MORRIS

WHEN THINGS GET TOO AWFUL, when the rain never seems likely to stop, and the toolmakers are striking, and Sam the dog has been rolling in manure—when life seems irredeemable, then I retreat to the lost world of my old guide-books. In that musty row of greens and browns all anxieties are sublimated, and nothing seems too dreadful. Fleas in Russia are only 'insects of a vexatory disposition.' Fish dishes in Egypt merely have 'a strong flavour of mud.' Danish white port wine is no more than 'a remarkable combination.' Dr. Vaume, the French physician of Crete, may be alarming in the flesh, but in Murray's *Handbook to Greece* (1884), he simply has 'the reputation of using violent remedies.' Camels will meet trains on request at Jungshahi, prices of walking dresses in the rue de la Paix may generally be reduced by a little bargaining and the third-class travelling community in the Rhenish Provinces, so Herr Baedeker assures us, is generally quiet and respectable.

The heyday of the guide-book was the nineteenth century, when steam had made travel relatively easy, but the average tourist was still an educated person, able to appreciate Murray's donnish quirks or Baedeker's obscurer allusions to the principles of Gothic fenestration. There are felicities, of course, to be found both in earlier and in later examples. My favourite guide-book chapter, on the whole, is Chapter XII of Horrebow's *Iceland* (1758), which is entitled 'Concerning Owls in Iceland', and which consists in its entirety of one phrase: 'There are no owls of any kind in the whole island.' The guide-book advice I most admire is given by E.M. Forster in his *Alexandria* (1922)— 'The best way to see it is to wander aimlessly about'—while one could hardly improve the opening to Chapter IV of Mrs. R.L. Devonshire's *Rambles in Cairo* (1931): 'Of all the medieval rulers of Egypt, Saladin alone enjoys the privilege of being remembered by Western readers.' In our own time Mr. David Piper has enriched the classic repertoire with his *Companion Guide to London* (1964): 'All buses cover the routes in both directions, a fact one may well forget in the heat of the moment'; and the authors of the *Michelin Guide to New York City* (1968) honour old traditions handsomely with their conclusions on the New York subway: 'Riding the subway is an exciting experience for visitors, but daily commuters who have had a chance to try the comforts of the Paris or Montreal metroes would probably prefer to ride on those silent and modern trains equipped with special steel cord tires of French manufacture.'

But generally when despondency impends it is to

nineteenth-century practitioners that I turn, and
this is largely I think because they are of the railway
age, and transport me through their vicarious
delights to the lilt of sleeping-car wheels and the
clickety-click of the permanent way—only broken by
the cries of the *douaniers* at Modane ('British
passengers not required to produce passports') or the
intrusions of the ticket collector at Wierzbolow
('Passengers are recommended to pay the difference
at St. Petersburg between 1st and 2nd class, which is
only 7rs. 84c.'). One of the grandest of the railway
manuals was the *Guide to the Great Siberian
Railway* (1900), published by the Imperial Ministry
of Ways and Communications in an English translation intended to lure English tourists and business-
men along the golden road to Vladivostok. This
stands on my shelves in a position preordained: next
door to Adam's and Bishop's *Complete Traveler*'s
*Guide of the Union and Central Pacific Rail-
roads* (1881), 'The Handsomest Guide-Book in the
World.'

No escape could be more utter than an hour
with these two illustrated books, side by side upon
the hearth. Both their worlds have vanished: the
Russia of 1900 so tentative, so defensive, so clamped
behind the frontispiece of His Imperial Majesty
Nicholas Alexandrovich, Autocrat of All the Russias
and Most August President of the Siberian Railway;
the America of 1881 so marvellously brash and
energetic, so full of hope, so innocently encapsulated

in this, 'The Most Complete, Accurate and Reliable Trans-Continental Guide Ever Known'—'far in advance', as Samuel Powell, General Ticket Agent of the Chicago, Burlington and Quincy Railroad, testifies, 'of any other work of similar character that has come to my notice.'

Take the trains themselves, into whose varnished and embossed compartments these volumes so vividly usher us. It is true that palace-car life on the Union Pacific looks more fun, at least in lithograph, with songs at the harmonium, mysterious Indians hovering around the spittoon, and a most comfortable and convenient eating-house to look forward to at Rock Creek, Wyoming. The week's journey from Chicago to the coast may well pass like a flash if, as the book suggests, we 'indulge in social conversation and glee.' But the Great Siberian Railway actually has a Church Car, with icons, tall candles, a priest in attendance and a cross on the roof: and no Pullman could match the listless Chekhovian dignity of the Great Siberian saloon, with its glass-fronted library shelves, its tasselled armchairs, its portraits of eminent railway engineers and its chessmen already laid out for play on the corner table beneath the clock.

From the windows of the Union Pacific one sees feathered Sioux, elks, beautiful cowboys, scenic wonders and the Family Residence of Brigham Young. From the windows of the Great Siberian one looks out upon a morose parade of Yakutsk, Ostyaks and landing-places on the Ob. The hotel at Cheyenne depot is hung with the heads of black-tailed deer, 'all nicely preserved and looking very natural', but the station at Olginskaya looks like the pavilion of some exceptionally prosperous bowling club, or perhaps a small casino. The Union Pacific guide has a picture of a venerable engine-driver leaning from his cab to kiss an infant a whiskery good-bye. The *Guide to the Great Siberian Railway* contains a message from the All Highest: 'Gentlemen! To have begun the construction of the railway line across Siberia is one of the greatest achievements of my never to be forgotten Father. The fulfilment of this essentially peaceful work, entrusted to me by my beloved Father, is my sacred duty and my sincere desire.'

Yet both books are, in their disparate ways, expressions of Manifest Destiny. The aftertaste of such old convictions, so urgent or majestic in their time, now harmless or discredited, is for the real *aficionado* a peculiar delicacy of old guide-books.

Another is a sense of transference, the power Murray and Baedeker possess to deposit you in the shoes of your great-grandparents, to see the world with their eyes, dip into their capacious bags for Gratuities or Cockle's Pills ('if not used by oneself, they are useful to give to servants or villagers'), or make it clear to the manager of the Hotel Dagmar that you will not put up, as so many travellers in Denmark are obliged to, with damp table napkins.

The English guides are best for this. They make one feel gloriously assured. Herr Baedeker can be scathing enough about the performances of Egyptian clowns—'disgracefully insolent'—or the morals of Neapolitan innkeepers—'The traveller is often tempted to doubt whether such a thing as honesty is known here': but for sheer superbia, for the exhilaration of *noblesse oblige*, the English nineteenth-century guide-book stands alone. There are disappointments, of course. T. Bennett in *Handbook for Norway* (1878) tells us abjectly that because so many foolish things are written by British travellers in railway suggestion books, the authorities seldom pay any attention to remarks entered in English: but then Mr. Bennett, the doyen of Norwegian tourism, lives in Christiana himself and is probably demoralized by intimate contact with natives. Far more characteristic is Mr. Hare's Augustan dismissal of Venetian guides: 'All but the most hopelessly imbecile travellers will find them an intolerable nuisance', or Murray's noble reassurance to British visitors in Athens: 'Any Englishman having the usual knowledge of ancient Greek will be able to read the Athenian papers with ease.'

For it is true, I fear, that the best guide-books,

like the best travel books, are generally written by resolute outsiders—observers who preserve the integrity of detachment, and write first of all to their own satisfaction. Americans are bad at this, feeling in themselves a necessity to integrate, which is why they so often produce ingratiating guides and ineffable books of travel: but our British fore-bears, secure in the extraordinary good fortune of their nationality and the inestimable advantage of a classical education, were very good at it indeed. They were seldom so mean as to be curmudgeonly, but they felt no need to be fulsome. This was the Eothen vein, which was worked skilfully into our own times by Robert Byron and Peter Fleming, but which displayed its richest lode in the travel litera-ture of mid-Victorian Britain.

The greatest guide-book of all is Murray's *Handbook for Spain* (1845), which is the master-piece of Richard Ford, and one of the best books of any kind about Spain. Transference to the plane of this work is the perfect stimulant, for never was there so racy, so exuberant, so learned, so marvel-lously uninhibited a traveller as Ford. In his company, one feels, nothing can go wrong for long, and boredom is impossible. The Valencians may well be perfidious, vindictive, sullen, mistrustful, fickle, treacherous, smooth, empty of all good, snarling and biting like hyenas and smiling as they murder, but dear Richard's charm will soon win them over: as for the Spanish smuggler, that swaggering MacHeath of Andalusia, a cigar and a *bota* of wine will soon open his heart, and anyway he likes and trusts an Englishman—'not that he won't rob him if in want of cash.'

Ford is often rude, but, because he cares for nobody's opinion, never priggish or patronizing. His exasperations are always redeemed by humour; his admiration is as generous as his contempt is unsparing. One feels in his presence that the best guide-books are far more than informational aides, more even than literature, but are manuals of sensibility. When I travel with Richard Ford, if only in the privacy of my own library, I assume not merely his vision and hearing, but his feelings too: I am brightened in myself by his gaiety, enriched by his scholarship, mellowed by his kindness. Travel in a foreign country, especially perhaps such a country as Spain in the 1840s, should exercise every faculty: like a Finnish sauna or Eng. Lit. at Cambridge, it ought to be an awakening of all our powers, and an invitation to experiences that require no Steamship Reservations or Changes of Train at all.

This is the gift of the best of these English guides: to give to the reader even now something of the potency, the alertness and the dash that went with Victorian England's convictions of merit. There is nothing like it, I find, after the ten o'clock news.

Yet I cannot deny that half the pleasures of my old guide-books are physical. I love them as objects. I have in my shelves a facsimile edition of Baedeker's English *Guide to Russia*. It is a handsome replica, and provides an unequalled diagram of Russia in the last years of the monarchy: but though I admit it is handy to know that Matins in the English Church at Riga is at 11 a.m., and comforting to be told that the Girls' Friendly Society maintains a hostel in Odessa, still I think I shall always cherish more dearly my original German version of the book, whose pages are yellowing, whose maps are ragged at the edges, and which I bought one icy November morning in the Nevski Prospekt—empty, alas, of the scarlet-liveried carriages and Tartar old-clothes pedlars recommended to me inside.

For all the magic of the old guides cannot be reproduced. It is only partly in their words; the rest is embodied in their smell of age and foreign ink, the suggestion of salt-spray on their bindings, the spindly signatures of their previous owners, or the faded pink Ticket of Admittance, tucked still within the museum itinerary, which, like a madeleine dipped in tea, can evoke so miraculously other times in distant places.

—1976

The Diary

By SAMUEL PEPYS

8 *February*.

AWAY TO THE STRAND to my booksel-ler's, and there stayed an hour and bought that idle, roguish book, *L'Escholle des Filles*; which I have bought in plain binding (avoiding the buying of it better bound) because I resolve, as soon as I have read it, to burn it, that it may not stand in the list of books, nor among them, to disgrace them if it should be found.

9 *February*. *Lord's Day*.

Up, and at my chamber all the morning and the office, doing business and also reading a little of *L'Escholle des Filles*, which is a mighty lewd book, but yet not amiss for a sober man once to read over to inform himself in the villainy of the world. At noon home to dinner, where by appointment Mr Pelling came, and with him three friends: Wallington that sings the good bass, and one Rogers, and a gentleman, a young man, his name Tempest, who sings very well endeed and understands anything in the world at first sight. After dinner, we into our dining room and there to singing all the afternoon. We sang till almost night, and drank my good store of wine; and then they parted and I to my chamber, where I did read through *L'Escholle des Filles*; a lewd book, but what doth me no wrong to read for information sake (but it did hazer my prick para stand all the while, and una vez to decharger); and after I had done it, I burned it, that it might not be among my books to my shame; and so at night to supper and then to bed.

—1668

From a Letter

By *FRANCESCO PETRARCH*

ONE UNQUENCHABLE LONGING has the mastery of me, which hitherto I neither could nor would repress; for I flatter myself that a desire for things honourable is no dishonour. The malady I mean is an insatiable craving for books, although, perhaps, I already have more than I ought. While with books, as with other things, success only augments cupidity, yet with books there is something peculiar. Gold, silver, jewels, purple raiment, fine houses, broad acres, paintings, caparisoned steeds, afford a dumb and superficial pleasure. Books, however, delight us to the marrow; they advise us and talk with us and treat us with a bright and witty familiarity. Nor does each ingratiate itself by its own merit alone, but suggests the names of more, and one begets a desire for another. For example, the *Academics* of Cicero endeared to me Marcus Varro; from the *De Officiis* I first heard the name of Ennius; the *Tusculan Disputations* first imbued me with the love of Terence. . . .

"It is no marvel then (to return from my digression) if books enkindle and inflame our minds, both openly by their own warmth and attractiveness, and secretly by furnishing the names of others contained in them. So I frankly and truthfully confess

—though I blush for it—that the coveting of them
first by Pisistratus, afterwards by Ptolemy Philadel-
phus appears to me nobler than the avarice of Cras-
sus, despite the fact that the latter has many more
imitators. But there is no ground for Alexandria or
Athens—for Egypt or Greece—to exult over Rome
and Italy. We, too, have had our learned Emperors
—so many that it is hard even to count them—so
devoted to study that there was one to whom philosophy was dearer than Empire—men, I say, who loved
not books in themselves, but rather their contents.
(There are some, of course, who amass books not for
use but from the lust of possession—not as an assistance to their wits, but as an ornament to their
rooms.) To pass over others, the 'divine' Julius and
Augustus made provisions for a Roman Library; the
former set over it Marcus Varro—a man (with all
deference to Demetrius Phalereus, of whom the
Egyptians thought so highly) in no way his inferior,
but rather far above him; the latter appointed Pom-
peius Macer, a man of great learning. Asinius Pollio,
the celebrated orator, was most enthusiastic about
his Greek and Latin library; and he was the first to
throw one open to the public at Rome. And there
are other private instances; there is Cato's insatiable
hunger for books, to which Cicero bears witness, and
there is the ardour of the orator himself in sending
for them—testified in so many letters to Atticus,
whom he urges to the task with as much insistence
and entreaty as I am employing towards you. If a

man of such rich endowments submits to 'hand the hat round' for such a purpose, what may not be permitted to a beggar?

"Let this be an excuse for my offence; I have at least the comfort of famous companions in crime. If you love me, lay this charge upon a few trusty and lettered men. Let them ransack Tuscany, and turn over the chests of the religious orders and other studious persons, to see if anything can be found to appease or (shall I say?) to whet my thirst. Finally, though you are aware in what lakes I am wont to fish and in what woods I go a hawking, yet—that there may be no mistake—I enclose in this letter a separate list of my chief 'desiderata'; and to make you keep a closer watch, let me tell you that I have addressed the same entreaties to other friends in Britain, France, and Spain. Pray do your utmost not to yield to them in faith and diligence."

—1346

Marginalia

By *EDGAR ALLAN POE*

IN GETTING MY BOOKS, I have been always solicitous of an ample margin; this not so much through any love of the thing in itself, however agreeable, as for the facility it affords me of pencilling suggested thoughts, agreements, and differences of opinion, or brief critical comments in general. Where what I have to note is too much to be included within the narrow limits of a margin, I commit it to a slip of paper, and deposit it between the leaves; taking care to secure it by an imperceptible portion of gum tragacanth paste.

All this may be whim; it may be not only a very hackneyed, but a very idle practice;—yet I persist in it still; and it affords me pleasure; which is profit, in despite of Mr. Bentham, with Mr. Mill on his back.

This making of notes, however, is by no means the making of mere *memoranda*—a custom which has its disadvantages, beyond doubt. "*Ce que je mets sur papier*," says Bernadine de St. Pierre, "*je remets de ma memoire et par consequence je l'oublie;*"—and, in fact, if you wish to forget anything upon spot, make a note that this thing is to be remembered.

But the purely marginal jottings, done with no eye to the Memorandum Book, have a distinct complexion, and not only a distinct purpose, but none at all; this it is which imparts to them a value. They have a rank somewhat above the chance and desultory comments of literary chit-chat—for these latter are not unfrequently "talk for talk's sake," hurried out of the mouth; while the *marginalia* are deliberately pencilled, because the mind of the reader wishes to unburthen itself of a *thought*;—however flippant—however silly—however trivial—still a thought indeed, not merely a thing that might have been a thought in time, and under more favorable circumstances. In the *marginalia*, too, we talk only to ourselves; we therefore talk freshly—boldly—originally—with *abandonnement*—without conceit—much after the fashion of Jeremy Taylor, and Sir Thomas Browne, and Sir William Temple, and the anatomical Burton, and that most logical analogist, Butler, and some other people of the old day, who were too full of their matter to have any room for their manner, which, being thus left out of question, was a capital manner, indeed,—a model of manners, with a richly marginalic air.

The circumscription of space, too, in these pencillings, has in it something more of advantage than of inconvenience. It compels us (whatever diffuseness of idea we may clandestinely entertain), into Montesquieu-ism, into Tacitus-ism (here I leave out of view the concluding portion of the "Annals") —or even into Carlyle-ism—a thing which, I have been told, is not to be confounded with your ordinary affectation and bad grammar. I say "bad grammar," through sheer obstinacy, because the grammarians (who should know better) insist upon it that I should not. But then grammar is not what these grammarians will have it; and, being merely the analysis of language, with the result of this analysis, must be good or bad just as the analyst is sage or silly—just as he is Horne Tooke or a Cobbett.

But to our sheep. During a rainy afternoon, not long ago, being in a mood too listless for continuous study, I sought relief from *ennui* in dipping here and there, at random, among the volumes of my library—no very large one, certainly, but sufficiently miscellaneous; and, I flatter myself, not a little *recherche*.

Perhaps it was what the Germans call the "brain-scattering" humor of the moment; but, while the picturesqueness of the numerous pencil-scratches arrested my attention, thcir helter-skelter-iness of commentary amused me. I found myself at length forming a wish that it had been some other hand than my own which had so bedevilled the books, and fancying that, in such case, I might have derived no inconsiderable pleasure from turning them over. From this the transition-thought (as Mr. Lyell, or Mr. Murchison, or Mr. Featherstonhaugh would have it) was natural enough:—there might be something even in *my* scribblings which, for the mere sake of scibbling, would have interest for others.

The main difficulty respected the mode of transferring the notes from the volumes—the context from the text—without detriment to that exceedingly frail fabric of intelligibility in which the context was imbedded. With all appliances to boot, with the printed pages at their back, the commentaries were too often like Dodona's oracles—or those of Lycophron Tenebrosus—or the essays of the pedant's pupils, in Quintilian, which were "necessarily excellent, since even he (the pedant) found it impossible to comprehend them":—what, then, would become of it—this context—if transferred?—if translated? Would it not rather be *traduit* (traduced) which is the French synonym, or *overzezet* (turned topsy-turvy) which is the Dutch one?

I concluded, at length, to put extensive faith in the acumen and imagination of the reader:—this as a general rule. But, in some instances, where even faith would not remove mountains, there seemed no safer plan than so to re-model the note as to convey at least the ghost of a conception as to what it was all about. Where, for such conception, the text itself was absolutely necessary, I could quote it; where the title of the book commented upon was indispensable, I could name it. In short, like a novel-hero dilemma'd, I made up my mind "to be guided by circumstances," in default of more satisfactory rules of conduct.

As for the multitudinous opinion expressed in the subjoined *farrago*—as for my present assent to all, or dissent from any portion of it—as to the possibility of my having, in some instances, altered my mind— or as to the impossibility of my not having altered it often—these are points upon which I say nothing, because upon these there can be nothing cleverly said. It may be as well to observe, however, that just as the goodness of your true pun is in the direct ratio of its intolerability, so is nonsense the essential sense of the Marginal Note. . . .

—1844

Reading

By HENRY DAVID THOREAU

MY RESIDENCE WAS MORE favorable, not only to thought, but to serious reading, than a university; and though I was beyond the range of the ordinary circulating library, I had more than ever come within the influence of those books which circulate round the world, whose sentences were first written on bark, and are now merely copied from time to time onto linen paper. Says the poet Mir Camar Uddin Mast, "Being seated to run through the region of the spiritual world; I have had this advantage in books. To be intoxicated by a single glass of wine; I have experienced this pleasure when I have drunk the liquor of the esoteric doctrines." I kept Homer's Iliad on my table through the summer, though I looked at his page only now and then. Incessant labor with my hands, at first, for I had my house to finish and my beans to hoe at the same time, made more study impossible. Yet I sustained myself by the prospect of such reading in future. I read one or two shallow books of travel in the intervals of my work, till that employment made me ashamed of myself, and I asked where it was then that *I* lived.

The student may read Homer or Aeschylus in the Greek without danger of dissipation or luxuriousness, for it implies that he in some measure emulate their heroes, and consecrate morning hours to their pages. The heroic books, even if printed in the character of our mother tongue, will always be in a language dead to degenerate times; and we must laboriously seek the meaning of each word and line, conjecturing a larger sense than common use permits out of what wisdom and valor and generosity we have. The modern cheap and fertile press, with all its translations, has done little to bring us nearer to the heroic writers of antiquity. They seem as solitary, and the letter in which they are printed as rare and curious, as ever. It is worth the expense of youthful days and costly hours, if you learn only some words of an ancient language, which are raised out of the trivialness of the street, to be perpetual suggestions and provocations. It is not in vain that the farmer remembers and repeats the few Latin words which he has heard. Men sometimes speak as if the study of the classics would at length make way for more modern and practical studies; but the adventurous student will always study classics, in whatever language they may be written and however ancient they may be. For what are the classics but the noblest recorded thoughts of man? They are the only oracles which are not decayed, and there are such answers to the most modern inquiry in them as Delphi and Dodona never gave. We might as well omit to study Nature because she is old. To read well, that is, to read true books in a true spirit, is a noble exercise, and one that will task the reader more than any exercise which the customs of the day esteem. It requires a training such as the athletes underwent, the steady intention almost of the whole life to this object. Books must be read as deliberately and reservedly as they were written. . . .

. . . A written word is the choicest of relics. It is something at once more intimate with us and more universal than any other work of art. It is the work of art nearest to life itself. It may be translated into every language, and not only be read but actually breathed from all human lips; not be represented on canvas or in marble only, but be carved out of the breath of life itself. The symbol of an ancient man's thought becomes a modern man's speech. Two thousand summers have imparted to the monuments of Grecian literature, as to her marbles, only a maturer golden and autumnal tint, for they have carried their own serene and celestial atmosphere into all lands to protect them against the corrosion of time. Books are the treasured wealth of the world and the fit inheritance of generations and nations. Books, the oldest and the best, stand naturally and rightfully on the shelves of every cottage. They have no cause of their own to plead, but while they enlighten and sustain the reader his common sense will not refuse them. Their authors are a natural and irresistible aristocracy in every society, and, more than kings or emperors, exert an influence on mankind. When the illiterate and perhaps scornful trader has earned by enterprise and industry his coveted leisure and independence, and is admitted to the circles of wealth and fashion, he turns inevitably at last to those still higher but yet inaccessible circles of intellect and genius, and is sensible only of the imperfection of his culture and the vanity and insufficiency of all his riches, and further proves his good sense by the pains which he takes to secure for his children that intellectual culture whose want he so keenly feels; and thus it is that he becomes the founder of a family. . . .

The works of the great poets have never yet been read by mankind, for only great poets can read them. They have only been read as the multitude read the stars, at most astrologically, not astronomically. Most men have learned to read to serve a paltry convenience, as they have learned to cipher in order to keep accounts and not be cheated in trade; but of reading as a noble intellectual exercise they know little or nothing; yet this only is reading, in a high sense, not that which lulls us as a luxury and suffers the nobler faculties to sleep the while, but what we have to stand on tiptoe to read and devote our most alert and wakeful hours to.

I think that having learned our letters we should read the best that is in literature, and not be forever repeating our a b abs, and words of one syllable, in the fourth or fifth classes, sitting on the lowest and foremost form all our lives. Most men are satisfied if they read or hear read, and perchance have been convicted by the wisdom of one good book, the Bible, and for the rest of their lives vegetate and dissipate their faculties in what is called easy reading. There is a work in several volumes in our Circulating Library entitled Little Reading, which I thought referred to a town of that name which I had not been to. There are those who, like cormorants and ostriches, can digest all sorts of this, even after the fullest dinner of meats and vegetables, for they suffer nothing to be wasted. If others are the machines to provide this provender, they are the machines to read it. . . .

. . . How many a man has dated a new era in his life from the reading of a book! The book exists for us perchance which will explain our miracles and reveal new ones. The at present unutterable things we may find somewhere uttered. These same questions that disturb and puzzle and confound us have in their turn occurred to all the wise men; not one has been omitted; and each has answered them, according to his ability, by his words and his life. Moreover, with wisdom we shall learn liberality. The solitary hired man on a farm in the outskirts of Concord, who has had his second birth and peculiar religious experience, and is driven as he believes into silent gravity and exclusiveness by his faith, may think it is not true; but Zoroaster, thousands of years ago, traveled the same road and had the same experience; but he, being wise, knew it to be universal, and treated his neighbors accordingly, and is even said to have invented and established worship among men.

184

Let him humbly commune with Zoroaster then, and through the liberalizing influence of all the worthies, with Jesus Christ himself, and let "our church" go by the board. . . .

—1854

The Bookworm

By GORDON WILSON

I WAS SHIPPED INTO the division when it was in training in the desert. I had brought only one book with me. I finished it soon, and then I couldn't find any others. I had never been anywhere where books weren't available, and it didn't occur to me that I could live without them.

I looked everywhere, and I settled for reading a dictionary that I borrowed from the message center. I started out reading it straight through word by word, but I was skipping around even before I got through A section. Somebody told me that there was a private named Graffington who had a lot of books. Graffington was on the third hill over, and you could tell his foxhole because it was the deepest one in the whole company. I took my book, *Madame Bovary*, and hiked over to the hill, but I couldn't find Private Graffington. Somebody said he might be on the next hill. I went there, but I was told there to try another hill. I went there and found a deep foxhole, the deepest that I had ever seen in the company. There was nobody in it. I got down into it and found books under a blanket, a set of Shakespeare in thin volumes and an anthology of poems. I climbed back out.

A soldier came walking up the hill. When the

soldier got closer I saw that he had to be the owner of the books. I didn't keep from saying it: "Private Graffington, I presume." Standing tall, we shook hands. I told him my problem and offered *Madame Bovary* to him. He said: "I've never read Flaubert, and it's time I began. Please come in." His foxhole was big enough to hold two men comfortably. He uncovered his books and said: "Take your pick. Take as many as you like."

I was afraid that we wouldn't be supplied with books when we went overseas, and I thought that I had better take some with me. There was a limit on what we could take, and I went far beyond it. I sewed some of the books into the lining of my overcoat, but I still had too many books in my duffel bag. We came to a company formation at which we lined up with our duffel bag to get on the train to go to the port of embarkation, and I couldn't get my bag closed.

Sergeant Morton put on a show of having two men help me stamp down the bag. Sergeant Morton dramatized it so much that the whole company became aware of it. After we finally got it closed, Sergeant Morton came over to me and said: "You get the next shit detail." Sergeant Morton was a bully who had to pick on somebody, and he picked especially on me and Private Graffington. We were new to the outfit and had no rank, and Sergeant Morton held our book reading against us, especially the kind of books we read.

When we got on the train we had to do it
according to a careful plan because it was going to
be so overcrowded. If you were the second man into
a seat, you gave the first man your overcoat to stash
away in the allotted place. I happened to be the
second man, and I gave my coat to the first man.
The extra weight of the books sewed into the lining
caught him by surprise, and he dropped the coat
and said: "goddam."

Sergeant Morton came up the aisle. He didn't
say anything. He just held out his hand for the
coat. He went out with it, and after a while he
brought it back. The linings were cut and the books
were gone. He said: "I promise you. I promise you.
This goddam idiot sewed up a bunch of his goddam
books in his goddam overcoat. We're gonna get on
a boat and there won't be much to do for a while,
but we're gonna get off the boat, and then I
promise you."

Sergeant Morton came into the tent in the camp
in England and pointed to me. "I made you a
promise. Back in the States I made you a promise."

It was the honeybucket detail. I had to help the
English farmboy empty the honeybuckets into his
tank wagon. In that camp the soldiers defecated into
buckets, and then the English farmers would come
around and empty the buckets into their manure
wagons. For five hours that day I had to go around
the camp with the farmboy and empty the honey-

buckets, pick them up and lift them up and pour them out into the wagon, one by one, dozens of them.

It was during the early days in France. I was outside washing out my socks and underwear when Private Graffington came and told me what Sergeant Morton was up to. Sergeant Morton was talking about getting rid of junk and getting into my books. Sergeant Morton's excuse was an order from the company commander that the company was to travel lighter and get rid of non-essential things. I had already got rid of some of my books and had only about ten left. The company was still lugging plenty of things for other people too, accordions, guitars, horseshoes, baseball bats, and other things.

When I came into the room, there were a lot of people there, and Sergeant Morton was putting on a show of burning books in the stove. I went right up to him, and he wasn't expecting that. I grabbed *Moby Dick* out of his hand. I put the book back into the box and said: "Try to burn another one, and I'll knock your goddam teeth down your goddam throat."

Sergeant Morton did not move on the books, and it was a little while before he said anything. "We're not gonna carry that crap around any more. We're getting rid of it."

I said: "Never on your orders, you son of a bitch. You goddam yellow-bellied son of a bitch.

Tell you what. You persuade me. You just come outside for a few minutes and persuade me."

First Sergeant Kelly and Sergeant Blotion got between us and tried to calm things down. I grew hotter, though. "All I ask is five minutes with this son of a bitch. Just five minutes. And if I can't have that, get me out of this outfit. Just get me out of here, anywhere. Even a line company. I'd rather be in a line company than anywhere near this son of a bitch." But finally I allowed them to calm me down. I picked up the box of books and marched out of the room.

—1980

ABOUT THE EDITOR

Marshall Brooks was born in Neptune, New Jersey, in 1953 and raised in Newton, Massachusetts. Involved in literary publishing for over 25 years, he has published articles in numerous publications, including the *Boston Globe*, *Worcester Telegram*, *New York Times*, *Canadian Literature*, *Home Planet News*, and *Generalist Papers*. He is the author of *A Visit to Pinky Ryder*'s and editor of *Blackness of a White Night*, *Stories and Poems*, by Sherry Mangan. In 1979 Mr. Brooks established Arts End Books, a literary arts press.

Among the most curious titles in his personal library is *Survey of a Thousand Years of Beekeeping in Russia*, by Dorothy Galton; the most oft-consulted, Thoreau's *Journals* (the most recent memorable topic researched therein: beards). Mr. Brooks possesses 10 library cards.

The editor lives in Spencer, Massachusetts, with his wife, Stephanie, and two sons, Isaac and Graham, and can often be found consulting *Books in Print* at the hospitable town library there.